Sedley Taylor

Sound and Music

A Non-Mathematical Treatise on the Physical Constitution of Musical Sounds and

Harmony

Sedley Taylor

Sound and Music
A Non-Mathematical Treatise on the Physical Constitution of Musical Sounds and Harmony

ISBN/EAN: 9783337425050

Printed in Europe, USA, Canada, Australia, Japan

Cover: Foto ©Thomas Meinert / pixelio.de

More available books at **www.hansebooks.com**

SOUND AND MUSIC:

A NON-MATHEMATICAL TREATISE ON THE
PHYSICAL CONSTITUTION OF

Musical Sounds and Harmony,

INCLUDING

*THE CHIEF ACOUSTICAL DISCOVERIES OF
PROFESSOR HELMHOLTZ.*

BY

SEDLEY TAYLOR, M.A.
LATE FELLOW OF TRINITY COLLEGE, CAMBRIDGE.

London:
MACMILLAN AND CO.
1873.

[*All Rights reserved.*]

TO

SIR WILLIAM STERNDALE BENNETT

(PRINCIPAL),

AND TO THE

PROFESSORS AND STUDENTS,

OF THE

ROYAL ACADEMY OF MUSIC,

THIS VOLUME IS, WITH SINCERE RESPECT, DEDICATED.

PREFACE.

THE following treatise, portions of which have been delivered in lectures at the South Kensington Museum, the Royal Academy of Music, and elsewhere, aims at placing before persons unacquainted with Mathematics an intelligible and succinct account of that part of the Theory of Sound which constitutes the physical basis of the Art of Music. No preliminary knowledge, save of Arithmetic and of the musical notation in common use, is assumed to be possessed by the reader. The importance of combining theoretical and experimental modes of treatment has been kept steadily in view throughout.

The author has incorporated the chief Acoustical discoveries of Professor Helmholtz, but adopted his own course in explaining them and developing their connection with the previously established portions of the subject. The present volume, therefore, even where its obligations to the great German philosopher are the deepest, is not a mere epitome of his work [1], but the result of independent study.

TRINITY COLLEGE, CAMBRIDGE,
June, 1873.

[1] *Die Lehre von den Tonempfindungen. Dritte Ausgabe. Braunschweig.* 1870. Of this profound and exhaustive treatise it is not too much to say that it does for Acoustics what the *Principia* of Newton did for Astronomy.

CONTENTS.

CHAPTER I.

ON SOUND IN GENERAL, AND THE MODE OF ITS TRANSMISSION.

Sensation of Sound, and its cause, § 1—Connection of Sound with motion, § 2—Velocity of Sound, § 3—Stationary media of Sound, § 4—Motion of sea-waves, § 5—Description of a wave, § 6—Length, amplitude, and form of wave, § 7—Length of wave and time of vibration, § 8—Periodic vibrations, §§ 9, 10—Form of wave and mode of vibration, §§ 11, 12—Extension of term 'wave' to solid bodies, § 13—Wave on the surface of a field of standing corn, § 14—Longitudinal vibrations, §§ 15, 16—Condensation and rarefaction, § 17—Associated wave, § 18—Law of pendulum-vibration, § 19—Pressure and density of air; *Mariotte's* law, § 20—Transmission of sonorous waves along a tube of uniform bore, § 21—Unconstrained motion of Sound-waves, § 22—Musical and non-musical Sounds, § 23.

CHAPTER II.

ON LOUDNESS AND PITCH.

Three elements of a musical sound, loudness, pitch, and quality, § 24—Loudness and extent of vibration, § 25—Pitch and rapidity of vibration; the Syren; continuity of pitch, §§ 26, 27—Measure of pitch; vibration-numbers, § 28—Limits to the pitch of musical sounds, § 29—Relative pitch; intervals, § 30—Tonic intervals of the Major scale; concords and discords, § 31—Additional notes required for the Minor scale, 32—Measure of intervals, § 33—Vibration-fractions, § 34—Table of vibration-fractions for the tonic intervals of the Major and Minor scales, § 35—Calculation of the vibration-numbers of all the notes in a scale, from the vibration-number of its tonic, § 36.

CHAPTER III.

ON RESONANCE.

Resonating pianoforte wires and tuning-forks; cause of the phenomenon, §§ 37, 38—Resonance of a column of air; laws of its production, § 39—Relation between the length of an air-column and the pitch of its note of maximum resonance, § 40—Resonance-boxes, § 41—Helmholtz's resonators, § 42.

CHAPTER IV.

ON QUALITY.

Composite nature of musical sounds in general; series of constituent tones, and law which connects them, § 43—Experimental analysis of musical sounds, §§ 44, 45—Nomenclature of the subject, § 46—Helmholtz's theory of musical quality, as depending on the number, orders, and relative intensities of the partial-tones present in any given clang, § 47.

CHAPTER V.

ON THE ESSENTIAL MECHANISM OF THE PRINCIPAL MUSICAL INSTRUMENTS, CONSIDERED IN REFERENCE TO QUALITY.

Sounds of tuning-forks, § 48—Modes of vibration of an elastic tube, § 49—Meeting of equal and opposite pulses; formation of nodes, § 50—Number of nodes formed, § 51—Nature and rate of segmental vibration, §§ 52, 53—Motion of a sounding string; quality and pitch of its note, §§ 54, 55—The pianoforte, § 56—Meeting of equal and opposite systems of longitudinal waves, § 57—Reflection of Sound at a closed and at an open orifice, § 58—Modes of segmental vibration in stopped and open pipes, §§ 59, 60—Deepest note obtainable from a pipe, § 61—Relation between length of pipe and pitch of note, § 62—Theory of resonance-boxes, § 63—Flue-pipes and reed-pipes, § 64—Construction of flue-pipes and quality of their sounds, § 65—Mechanism of a reed; *timbre* of an independent reed, and of a reed associated with a pipe, § 66—Orchestral wind-instruments, § 67—Mechanism of the human voice, § 68—Synthetic confirmation of Helmholtz's theory of quality, § 69.

CHAPTER VI.

ON THE CONNECTION BETWEEN QUALITY AND MODE OF VIBRATION.

Composition of vibrations, § 70—Superposition of small motions § 71—Phase of a vibration; non-dependence of quality on differences of phase among partial-tones, § 72—Simple and resultant wave-forms; *Fourier's* theorem, § 73.

CHAPTER VII.

ON THE INTERFERENCE OF SOUND, AND ON 'BEATS.'

Composition of vibrations of equal periods, § 74—Two sounds producing silence, § 75—Beats of simple tones, § 76—Graphic representation of beats, § 77—Experimental study of beats, § 78.

CHAPTER VIII.

ON CONCORD AND DISCORD.

Helmholtz's discovery of the nature of dissonance; conditions under which it may arise between two simple tones, § 79—Mode of determining the whole dissonance produced by two composite sounds, § 80—Classification of the tonic intervals of the scale, according to their freedom from dissonance, §§ 81–86—Picture of amount of dissonance for all intervals not wider than one octave, § 87—Consonance dependent on quality, § 88—Apparent objection to Helmholtz's theory of quality, § 89—Combination-tones, § 90—Their use in defining certain consonant intervals for simple tones, § 91—Divergence from the views of musical theorists, § 92—Dissonance due to combination-tones produced between the partial-tones of clangs forming a given interval, § 93.

CHAPTER IX.

ON CONSONANT TRIADS.

Rules for the employment of vibration-fractions, §§ 94–96—Inversion of intervals, § 97—Definition of a consonant triad, § 98—Determination of all the consonant tonic triads within one octave, § 99—Major and Minor groups, § 100—Mutual relation between the members of each group, § 101—Notation of Thorough Bass, § 102—Fundamental and inverted positions of common chords, § 103—Effects of Major and Minor chords, § 104.

CHAPTER X.

ON PURE INTONATION AND TEMPERAMENT.

Successive intervals of the Major scale, § 105—Requisites for pure intonation in keyed instruments, §§ 106–108—Tempering and temperament, § 109—System of equal temperament, § 110—Its defects, § 111—Its influence on vocal intonation, § 112—Cumbrousness and inefficiency of the established pitch-notation for vocal music, § 113—The 'Tonic Sol-Fa' pitch-notation, § 114—Its simple and effective character, § 115—Relation of the physical theory of consonance and dissonance to the æsthetics of Music, § 116—Importance of extreme discords; conclusion, § 117.

SOUND AND MUSIC.

CHAPTER I.

ON SOUND IN GENERAL, AND THE MODE OF ITS TRANSMISSION.

1. IN listening to a Sound, all that we are immediately conscious of is a peculiar *sensation*. This sensation obviously depends on the action of our organs of hearing; for, if we close our ears the sensation is greatly weakened, or, if originally but feeble, altogether extinguished. Persons whose auditory apparatus is malformed, or has been destroyed by disease, may be totally unconscious of any sound, even during a thunder-storm, or the discharge of artillery. These simple considerations should prepare us to expect that what we feel as Sound may be represented, externally to ourselves, by a state of things very different to the sensation we experience. Indeed this would only be in accordance with the

modes of action of our other senses; for instance, the sensation of warmth, and its cause, a coal fire,—of fragrance, and its cause, a rose,—of pain, and its cause, a blow, are quite unlike each other. Analogy, then, indicates that some purely mechanical phenomena external to the ear will prove to be *turned into the sensation we call Sound* by a process carried on within that organ, and the brain with which it is in direct communication. This mechanical agency, whatever may be its nature, is usually set going at a distance from the ear, and, to reach it, must traverse the intervening space. In doing so, it can pass through solid and liquid as well as gaseous bodies. If one end of a felled tree is gently scratched with the point of a penknife, the sound is distinctly audible to a listener whose ear is pressed against the other end of the tree. When a couple of pebbles are knocked together under water, the sound of the blow reaches the ear after first passing through the intervening liquid. That Sound travels through the air is a matter of universal experience, and needs no illustration. In every case, accessible to common observation, where Sound passes from one point of space to another, it necessarily traverses *matter*, either in a solid, liquid, or gaseous form. We may hence conjecture that the presence of a material medium of some kind is indispensable to the transmission of Sound. This important point can be readily brought to the test of experiment, as follows. Let a bell, kept ringing by clockwork, be placed under the receiver of an air-pump, and the air gradually exhausted. Provided that suitable precautions are taken to prevent the communication of Sound through the base of the receiver itself, the bell will appear to ring more and more feebly as the exhaustion proceeds, until, at last, it altogether ceases to be heard. On re-admitting the air, the sound of the bell will gradually recover its original loudness. It results from this experiment that Sound cannot travel *in vacuo*, but requires for its transmission a material medium of some kind. The air of the atmosphere is, in the vast majority of cases, the medium which conveys to the ear the mechanical impulse which that wonderful organ *translates*, as it were, into the language of Sound.

2. Having ascertained that a material medium, in every case, acts as the carrier of Sound, we have next to examine in what manner it performs this function. The roughest observations suffice to put us on the right track, in this enquiry, by pointing to a connection between Sound and Motion. The passage, through the air, of sounds of very great intensity is accompanied by effects which prove the atmosphere to be in a state of violent commotion. The

explosion of a powder-magazine is capable of shattering the windows of houses at several miles' distance. Sounds of moderate loudness, such as the rattle of carriage-wheels, the stamping of feet, the clapping of hands, are produced by movements of solid bodies which cannot take place without setting up a very perceptible agitation of the air. In the case of weaker sounds, the accompanying air-motion cannot, it is true, be ordinarily thus recognized; but, even here, a little attention will usually detect a certain amount of movement on the part of the sound-producing apparatus, which is probably capable of being communicated to the surrounding air. Thus, a sounding pianoforte-string can be both seen and felt to be in motion: the movements of a finger-glass, stroked on the rim by a wet finger, can be recognized by observing the thrills which play on the surface of the water it contains: sand strewed on a horizontal drum head is thrown off when the drum is beaten. These considerations raise a presumption that Sound is *invariably* associated with agitation of the conveying medium—that it is impossible to produce a sound without at the same time setting the medium in motion. If this should prove to be the case, there would be ground for the further conjecture that motion of a material medium *constitutes* the mechanical impulse which, falling on the ear, excites within it the sensation we call Sound. Let us try to form an idea of the *kind* of motion which the conditions of the case require.

3. It will be convenient to begin by determining the *rate* at which Sound travels. This varies, indeed, with the nature of the conveying medium. It will suffice, however, for our present purpose to ascertain its velocity in *air*, the medium through which the vast majority of sounds reach our ears. As long as we confine our attention to sounds originating at but small distances from us, their passage through the intervening space appears instantaneous. If, however, a gun is fired at a considerable distance, the flash is seen before the report is heard—a proof that an appreciable interval of time is occupied by the transmission of the sound. The occurrence of an echo, in a position where we can measure the distance passed over by the sound in travelling from the position where it is produced to that where it rebounds, gives us the means of measuring the velocity of Sound; since we can, by direct observation, ascertain how long a time is spent on the out-and-home journey. The following easy experiment gives a near approximation to the actual velocity of Sound —in fact a much closer one than the rough nature of the observation would have led one to expect. In the North cloister of Trinity College, Cambridge,

there is an unusually distinct echo from the wall at its eastern extremity. Standing near the opposite end of the cloister, I clapped my hands rhythmically, in such a manner that the strokes and echoes succeeded each other alternately *at equal intervals of time*. A friend at my side, watch in hand, counted the number of strokes and echoes. The result was that there were 76 in half a minute, i.e. 38 strokes and 38 echoes. A little consideration will show that the sound traversed the cloister and returned to the point of its origination regularly once in each interval between a stroke and its echo. Since each such interval was exactly equal to that between an echo and the following stroke, the whole movement of Sound took place in alternate equal intervals, i.e. in half the observed time, or fifteen seconds. Accordingly the sound travelled *to and fro* in the cloister 38 times in 15 seconds. The length thus traversed, I found to be 419 feet. The velocity of Sound per second thus comes out equal to $\frac{38 \times 419}{15}$, or 1061[1] feet and a fraction. Sound, then, travels through the air at the rate of upwards of 1000 feet in a second, which is more than 600 miles an hour, or about 15 times the speed of an express-train. In solid and

---

[1] This is about 50 feet below its real value under the circumstances of my observation. See Tyndall's *Sound*, p. 24.

liquid bodies its velocity is still greater, attaining, in the case of steel-wire, a speed of from 15,000 to 17,000 feet in a second[1], or, roughly speaking, about 200 times that of an express-train.

4. Though the Sound-impulse thus advances with a steady and very high velocity, the medium by which it is transmitted clearly does not share such a motion. Solid conductors of Sound remain, on the whole, at rest during its passage, and a slight yielding of their separate parts is all that their constitution generally admits of. In fluids, or in the air, a rapid forward motion is equally out of the question. The movement of the particles composing the Sound-conveying medium will be found to be of a kind examples of which are constantly presenting themselves, but without attracting an amount of attention at all commensurate with their interest and importance.

5. An observer who looks down upon the sea from a moderate elevation, on a day when the wind, after blowing strongly, has suddenly dropped, sees long lines of waves advancing towards the shore at a uniform pace and at equal distances from each other. The effect, to the eye, is that of a vast army marching up in column, or of a ploughed field moving along

---

[1] Tyndall's *Sound*, p. 38.

horizontally in a direction perpendicular to the lines of its ridges and hollows. The *actual* motion of the water is, however, very different from its *apparent* motion, as may be ascertained by noticing the behaviour of a cork, or other body, floating on the surface of the sea, and therefore sharing its movement. Instead of steadily advancing, like the waves, the cork merely performs a heaving motion as the successive waves reach it, alternately riding over their crests and sinking into their troughs, as if anchored in the position it happens to occupy. Hence, while the waves travel steadily forward horizontally, the drops of water composing them are in a state of swaying to-and-fro motion, each separate drop rising and falling in a vertical straight line, but having no horizontal motion whatever[1].

Thus, when we say that the waves advance horizontally, we mean, not that the masses of water of which they at any given instant consist, advance, but that these masses, by virtue of the separate vertical motions of their individual drops, *successively arrange themselves in the same relative positions,* so that the curved shapes of the surface, which we call waves, are transmitted *without their materials sharing in the pro-*

---

[1] This statement, though not strictly accurate, is sufficiently near the truth for our present purpose. See Weber's *Wellenlehre*.

gress. The accompanying figure will show how this happens.

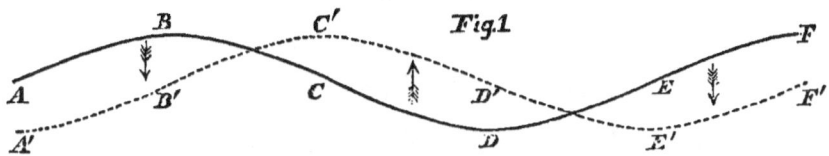

Let *ABCDEF* represent a section of a part of the sea-surface at any given instant, and suppose that during, say, the next ensuing second of time, the separate drops in *ABCDEF* move vertically, either upwards or downwards as shown by the arrows, so that, at the end of that second, they all occupy positions along the dotted curved line $A'B'C'D'E'F'$. The two portions, *ABCDE* and $B'C'D'E'F'$, are exactly alike, and, therefore, the effect is just what it would have been had we pushed the curve *ABCDE* along horizontally until it came to occupy the position $B'C'D'E'F'$.

In order further to illustrate this point, let us suppose that a hundred men are standing in a line and that the first ten are ordered to kneel down: a spectator who is too far off to distinguish individuals will merely see a broken line like that in the figure below.

Now, suppose that, after one second, the eleventh man is ordered to kneel and the first to stand; after two seconds the twelfth man to kneel and the second to stand; and so on. There will then continue to be a row of ten kneeling men, but, during each second, it will be shifted one place along the line. The distant observer will therefore see a depression steadily advancing along the line. The state of things presented to his eye after two, six, and nine seconds, respectively, is shown in Fig. 2.

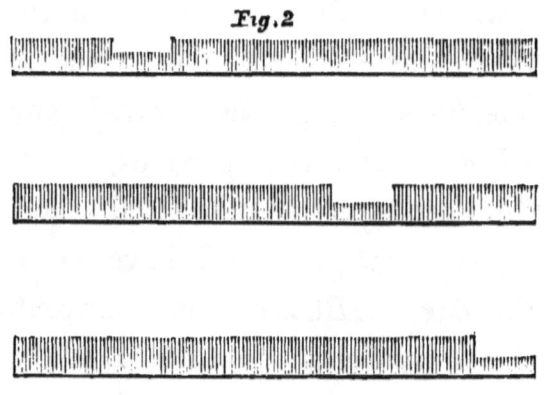

There is here no horizontal motion on the part of the men composing the line, but their vertical motions give rise, in the way explained, to the horizontal transference of the depression along the line. The reader should observe that for no two consecutive seconds does the kneeling row consist of exactly the same men, while in such positions as those shown in the figure, which are separated by more than ten seconds of time, the men who form it are totally different.

6. Let us now return to the sea-waves, and examine more closely the elements of which they consist.

Fig. 3 represents a vertical section of one complete wave.

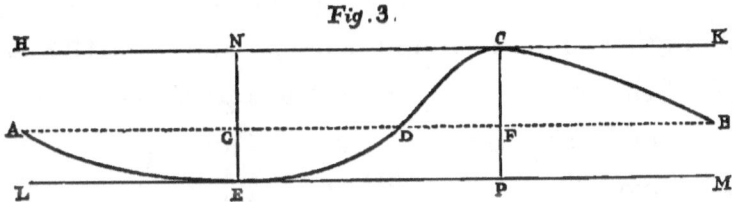

Fig. 3.

The dotted line is that in which the horizontal plane, forming the surface of the sea when at rest, cuts the plane of the figure. The distance between the two extreme points of the wave, measured along this line, is called the *length of the wave*. C is the highest point of the crest DCB; E the lowest point of the trough AED. CF and GE are vertical straight lines through C and E; HCK and LEM are horizontal straight lines through the same two points. The vertical distance between the lines HK and LM is called the *breadth* or *amplitude* of the wave. Thus AB is the length of the wave, and, if we produce EG and CF to cut the lines HK and

LM in N and P respectively, we have, for its amplitude, either of the equal lines EN, PC. Each of these is clearly equal to FC and GE together, that is to say, the amplitude of the wave is equal to the height of the crest above the level-line together with the depth of the trough below it. In addition to the length and amplitude of the wave, we have one more element, its *form*. The wave in the figure has its crest shorter than its trough and higher than its trough is deep. Moreover the part DC of the crest is steeper than the part CB, while, in the trough, the parts AE and EB are equally steep. Sea-waves have the most varied shapes according to the direction and force of the wind producing them. Hence, before we can lay down a wave in a figure, we must know the nature of the wave's curve, or, in other words, its form.

Since the crests of the waves are raised above the ordinary level of the sea, the troughs must necessarily be depressed below it, just as, in a ploughed field, the earth heaped up to form the ridges must be taken out of the furrows. Each crest being thus associated with a trough, it is convenient to regard one crest and one trough as forming together one complete wave. Thus each wave consists of a part raised above, and a part depressed below, the horizontal plane which would be the surface of the sea were it not being traversed by waves.

7. The *length, amplitude,* and *form* of a wave completely determine the wave, just as the length, breadth, and height of an oblong block of wood, i.e. its three dimensions, fix the size of the block. These three elements of a wave are mutually independent, that is to say, we may alter any one of them without altering the other two. This will be seen by a glance at the accompanying figures.

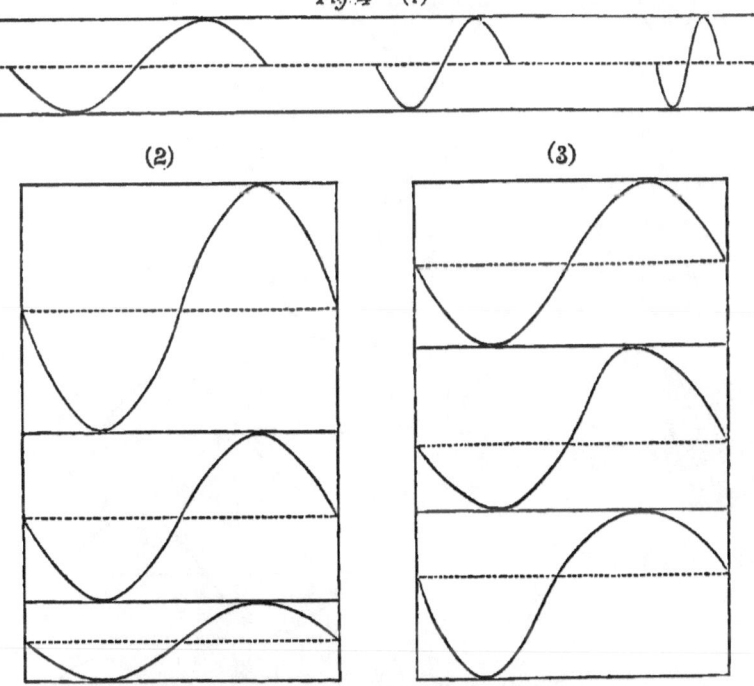

Fig. 4

(1) shows variation in *length* alone; (2) in *amplitude* alone; (3) in *form* alone.

14   DROP- AND WAVE-MOTION.   [I. § 7.

(1)

(2)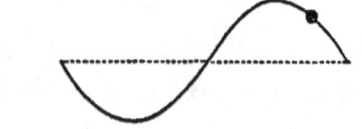

Fig. 5

(3)

(4)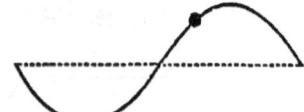

(5)

(6)

(7)

(8)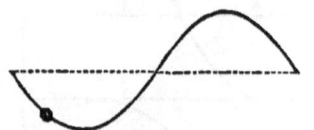

(9)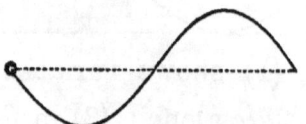

8. We will next study more closely the motion of an individual drop of water, in the surface of the sea, while a wave passes across it. Fig. 5 shows nine positions of the wave and moving drop at equal intervals of time, each one-eighth of the period during which the wave traverses a horizontal distance equal to its own wave-length. In (1), the front of the wave has just reached the drop previously at rest in the level-line represented by dots in the figure. In (2), the drop is a part of the way up the front of the crest; in (3), at the summit of the crest, and, therefore, at its greatest distance above the level-line. In (4), it is on the back of the crest, and, in (5), occupies its original position. It then crosses the level-line; is on the front of the trough in (6), and at its lowest point in (7), where it attains its greatest distance below the level-line. In (8), it is on the back of the trough, and, in (9), has once more returned to its starting-point in the level-line.

We have here a vibratory or oscillatory movement, like that of the end, or 'bob,' of a clock-pendulum, but executed in a vertical straight line. We call the distance between the two extreme positions of the bob, the extent of swing of the pendulum. The extent of the drop's oscillation will be seen, from (3) and (7), to be equal to the sum of the height of the wave's crest above the level-line, and of the depth of the trough below it.

But this, as was shown in § 6, is equal to the amplitude of the wave. Hence 'extent of drop's vibration' and 'amplitude of corresponding wave' are only different ways of expressing the same thing.

Let the line $A'OA$ be that in which the drop

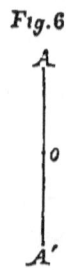

Fig. 6

under consideration vibrates, O being in the level-line, A and A' the limits of oscillation. The whole movement given in Fig. 5 will then be from O to A, from A through O to A', and from A' back again to O. This is termed *one complete vibration*, and since, in the course of it, each portion of the drop's path is passed over *twice*, one complete vibration is equal to an upward swing from A' to A together with a downward swing from A to A'. In the clock-pendulum we have, during each second, one complete oscillation, consisting of one swing from left to right and one from right to left.

Reference to Fig. 5 at once shows that, during the time occupied by the wave in traversing its own wave-length, the moving drop performs one complete vibration, or, to express the same fact in the reverse order, that *while the drop makes one complete vibration, the wave advances through one wave-length*. This is a most important principle, and should be thoroughly mastered and borne in mind by the student.

9. What has just been proved for a particular drop is, of course, equally true for *any* assigned drop in the surface passed over by a wave. All the drops, therefore, go through exactly the same vibrations in exactly equal times, but, since each drop can only start at the moment when the front of the wave reaches it [Fig. 5, (1)], they will in general occupy different positions in their paths at the same time. We may illustrate this by supposing a number of watches, which keep good time, to be set going successively in such a way that the first shall mark XII at twelve o'clock, the second at five minutes past twelve, the third at ten minutes past twelve, and so on. The hands of each watch will describe the same paths in equal times, but, at any assigned moment, will occupy different positions in those paths corresponding to the lateness of their several starts. The drops in the sea-

surface, being, in this manner, thrown *successively* into the same vibratory motion, give rise, by their consequent varieties of position at any assigned moment, to the transmission of the form which we call a wave.

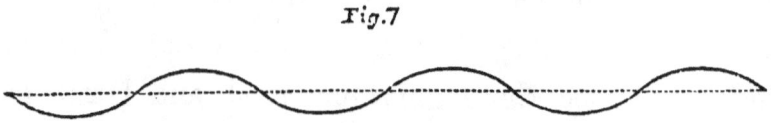

Fig. 7

When a series of continuous equal waves, such as those in Figure 7, are being transmitted, each oscillating drop, after completing one vibration, will instantly commence another precisely equal vibration, and go on doing so as long as the series of waves lasts. The kind of motion in which the same movement is continuously repeated in successive equal intervals of time, is called 'periodic,' and the time which any one of the movements occupies is called its 'period.' Thus, to continuous equal waves correspond continuous periodic drop-vibrations.

10. We will next compare the periods of the drop-vibrations corresponding to waves of *different lengths* advancing with *equal velocities*.

In Fig. 8 waves of three different lengths are represented. One wave of (1) is as long as two of (2), and as three of (3). Therefore a drop makes .

one complete vibration in (1) while the long wave passes from A to B, *two* in (2) while the shorter

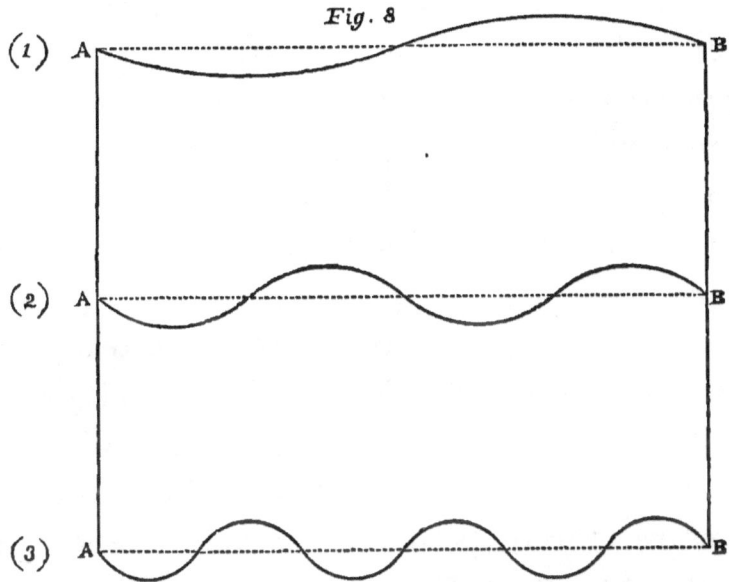

Fig. 8

waves there presented pass over the same distance, and *three* in the case of the shortest waves of (3). But the velocities of these waves being, by our supposition, equal, the times of describing the distance AB will be the same in (1), (2), and (3). Hence a drop in (2) vibrates twice as rapidly, and a drop in (3) three times as rapidly, as a drop in (1); or conversely, a drop in (1) vibrates half as rapidly as a drop in (2), and one third as rapidly as a drop in (3).

The *rates* of vibration in (1), (2) and (3), (by which we mean the numbers of vibrations performed in any given interval of time) are, therefore, proportional to the numbers 1, 2 and 3, which are themselves inversely proportional to the wave-lengths in the three cases, respectively. We may express our result thus; *the rate of drop-vibration is inversely proportional to the corresponding wave-length.* The same reasoning will apply equally well to any other case; the proposition, therefore, though derived from particular relations of wave-lengths, is true universally.

11. We have now connected the extent of the drop-vibration with the amplitude, and its rate with the length, of the corresponding wave. It remains to examine what feature of the oscillatory movement corresponds to the third element, the form, of the wave.

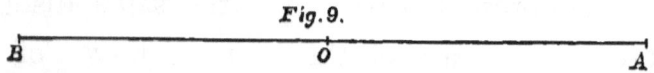

Fig. 9.

Suppose that two boys start together to run a race from O to A, from A to B, and from B back to O, and that they reach the goal at the same moment. They may obviously do this in many different ways. For instance, they may keep abreast all through, or one may fall behind over the first half of the course and recover the lost ground in the second. Again, one may be in front over OAO, and the other over OBO, or each boy may pass, and be passed by, his competitor, repeatedly during the race. We may regard the movement of each boy as constituting one complete vibration, and thus convince ourselves that an oscillatory motion of given *extent* and *period* may be performed in an indefinitely numerous variety of *modes*. Let us now compare the positions of a drop at successive equal intervals of time, when cooperating in the transmission of waves of different forms.

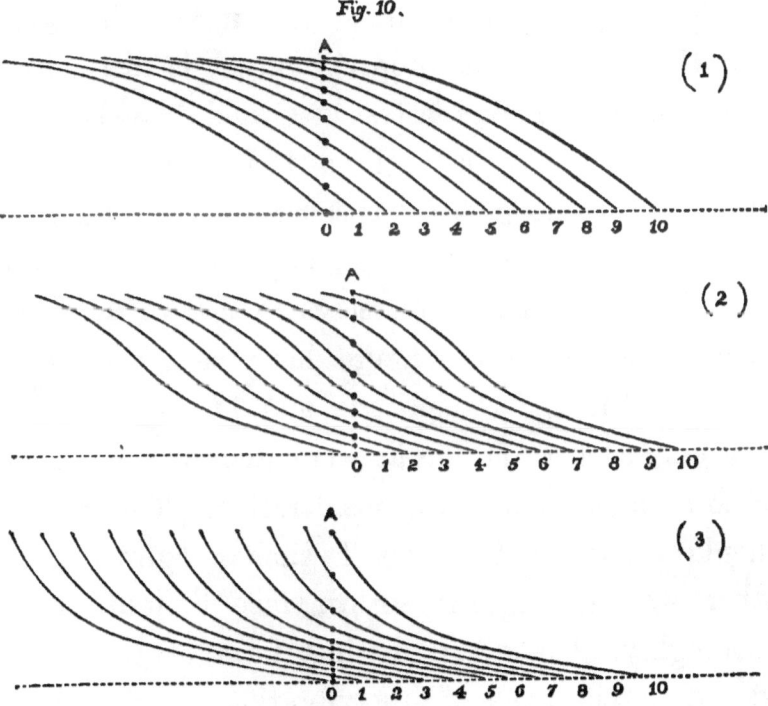

Fig. 10.

In each of the three cases in Fig. 10 the front of a wave-crest is shown in the positions it respectively occupies at the end of ten equal intervals of time (each one tenth of that occupied by the wave in traversing a quarter-wave-length), the apex of the wave being successively at the equidistant points of the level line 1, 2, 3, 4, &c.

A drop whose place of rest is O, will then assume the corresponding positions in the vertical line OA: thus the points where this line cuts the successive wave-fronts show the positions of the vibrating drop at equal intervals of time.

By comparing the three cases it will be seen that the mode of the drop's vibration is distinct in each. In (1), it moves fastest at O, and then slackens its pace up to A. In (2), it starts more slowly than in (1), attains its greatest speed near the middle of OA, and again slackens on approaching A. In (3), the pace steadily increases from O to A. The different waves in the figure have been purposely drawn of the same amplitude and length, in order that only such variations as were due to differences of form might come into consideration. The reader should construct for himself similar figures with other wave-forms, and so convince himself, more thoroughly, that every distinct form of wave has its own special mode of drop-vibration.

12. The converse of this proposition is also true, viz. that each distinct mode of drop-vibration gives rise to a special form of wave. We will show this by actually constructing the form of wave

which answers to a given mode of drop-vibration. When a drop vibrates in a given mode, its position at any assigned moment during its vibration is of course known. If we also know the amount by which drops further on in the level-line are *later in their starts* [§ 9] than drops less advanced in that line, we can assign the positions of any number of given drops at any given instant of time.

Suppose that each drop makes one complete vibration per second about its position of original rest in the level-line. The law of its vibration is roughly indicated in Fig. 11.

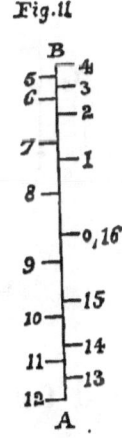

Fig. 11

AB is the path described by any drop; O its position when in the level line; 1, 2, 3, 4...16 its positions after 16 equal intervals of time each one-sixteenth of a second: 16 coincides with O, i.e. the drop has returned to its starting-point.

Next, select a series of drops originally at rest in equidistant positions along the level-line, and so situated that each commences a vibration, identical with that above laid down in Fig. 11, one-sixteenth of a second after the drop next it has started on an equal oscillation. Fig. 12 shows the rest-positions of the series of drops

$$a_0, \; a_1, \; a_2, \; a_3 \ldots a_{16},$$

in the level-line, and their contemporaneous positions

$$a_0, \; a_1', \; a_2', \; a_3' \ldots a_{16},$$

during a subsequent vibration.

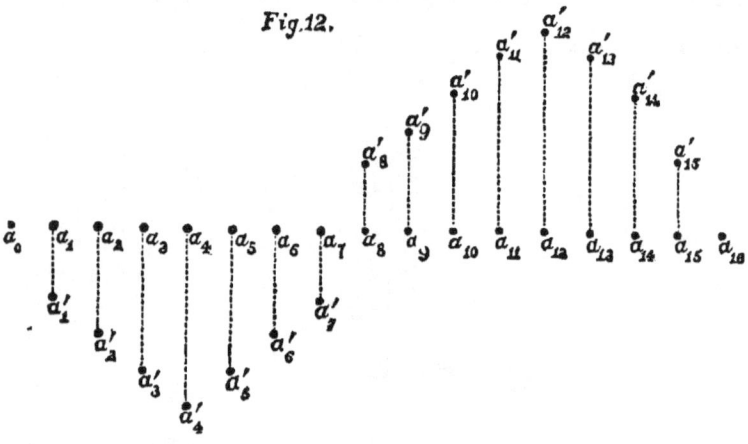

Fig. 12.

The moment selected for the figure is that in which the first of the series, a_0, is on the point of commencing its vibration in a vertical direction. Since the second drop started one-sixteenth of a second after the first, its position in the figure will be below the level-line at a_1' making the line

$a_1 a_1'$ equal to the line $O15$ in Fig. 11. The next drop, which is two-sixteenths behind a_0 in its path, will be at a_2' making $a_2 a_2'$ equal to $O14$ in the same figure. In this way the positions of all the points $a_1' a_2' a_3'$, &c., in Fig. 12 are determined from Fig. 11. They give us, at once, a general idea of the form of the resulting wave. By laying down more points along the line AB in Fig. 11, we can get as many more points on the wave as we please, and should thus ultimately arrive at a continuous curved line. This is the wave-form resulting from the given vibration-mode with which we started, and, since only one wave-form can be obtained from it, we infer that each distinct mode of drop-vibration gives rise to a special form of wave.

It has now been sufficiently shown that corresponding to the three elements of a wave, *amplitude, length,* and *form,* there are three elements of its proper drop-vibration, *extent, rate,* and *mode.*

13. We have seen that a sea-wave consists of a state of elevation and depression of the surface above and below the level-plane. The same thing holds of the small ripples set up by throwing a stone into a pond, and the non-progressive nature of the motion of individual drops on the surface can be as easily made out on a small, as on a large sheet of water. Moreover the characteristic phenomenon on which

we have been engaged, viz. *a uniformly progressive motion arising out of a number of oscillatory movements*, is by no means confined to liquid bodies. Thus, when a carpet is being shaken, bulging forms, exactly like water-waves, are seen running along it. A flexible string, one end of which is tied to a fixed point, and the other held in the hand, exhibits the same phenomenon when the loose end is suddenly twitched. It has accordingly been found convenient to extend the term 'wave' beyond its original meaning, and to designate as 'wave-motion' any movement which comes under the definition just laid down. We proceed to an instance of such motion which is important from its similarity to that to which the transmission of Sound is due.

14. Any one who has looked down from a slight elevation on a field of standing corn on a gusty day, must have frequently observed a kind of thrill running along its surface. As each ear of corn is capable of only a slight swaying movement, we have here necessarily an instance of *wave-motion*, the ear-vibrations corresponding to the drop-vibrations in water-waves. There is, however, this important difference between the cases, that the ears' movements are mainly horizontal, i. e. *in the line of the wave's advance*, whereas the drop-vibrations are entirely perpendicular to that line. The advancing wave

is therefore no longer exclusively a state of elevation or depression of surface, but of more tightly, or less tightly, packed ears. The annexed figure gives a

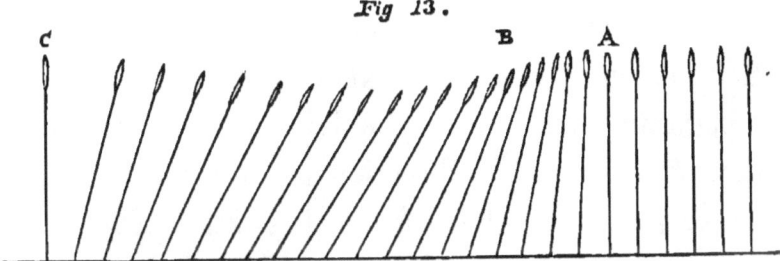

Fig 13.

rough idea how this takes place. The wind is supposed to be moving from left to right and to have just reached the ear A. Its neighbours to the right are still undisturbed. The stalk of C has just swung back to its erect position. The ears about B are closer to, and those about C further apart from, each other, than is the case with those on which the wind has not yet acted.

After this illustration, it will be easy to conceive a kind of wave-motion in which there is no longer (as in the case of the ears of corn) *any* movement transverse to the direction in which the wave is advancing.

15. Let a series of points, originally at rest in equidistant positions along a straight line, as in (0), Fig. 14, be executing equal periodic vibrations in that line, in such a manner that each point is a

certain fixed amount further back in its path than is its neighbour on *one* side, and therefore exactly as much more forward than is its neighbour on the *other* side.

(1) shows the condition of the row of points at the moment when the extreme point on the left is beginning its swing from left to right, which, in accordance with the direction of the arrow in the figure, we may call its forward swing. The equidistant vertical straight lines fix the extent of vibration for each oscillating point. The constant amount of retardation between successive points is, in the instance here selected, one-eighth of the path traversed by each point during the period of a complete oscillation. Thus, proceeding from left to right along the line (1), we have the first point beginning a forward swing, the second, third, fourth and fifth points entering respectively on the fourth, third, second, and first quarters of a backward swing, and the sixth, seventh, eighth and ninth points on the fourth, third, second, and first quarters of a forward swing.

Since the ninth point is just beginning a forward swing, its situation is exactly the same as that of the first point. Beyond this point, therefore, we have only repetitions of the state of things between the first and ninth points. The row (1) is therefore

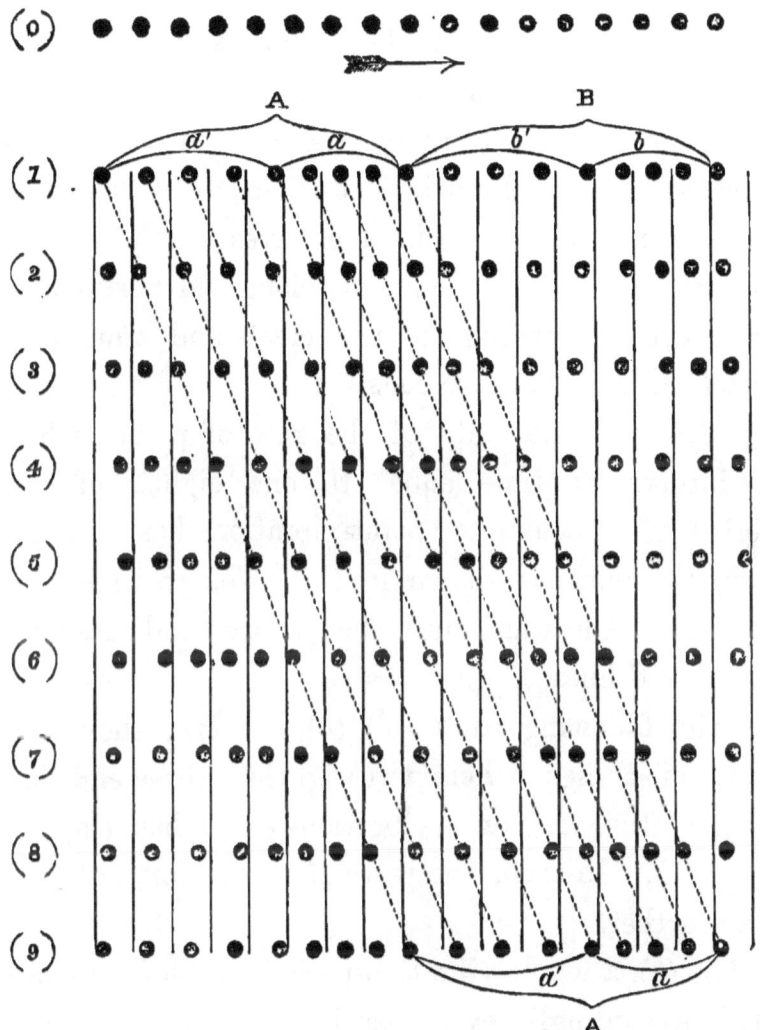

Fig. 14.

made up of a series of groups, or cycles, of the same number of points arranged in the same manner throughout. Two such cycles, included by the large brackets A and B, are shown in (1). Each cycle is divided by the small brackets a, a' and b, b' into two parts. In a and b the distances between successive points are less than, and in a' and b' greater than, the corresponding distances when the points occupied their undisturbed positions, as in (0). The cycles correspond to complete waves on the surface of water, the shortened and elongated portions of each cycle answering to the crest and trough of which each water-wave consists.

(2) shows the state of the row of points when an interval of time equal to one eighth of the period of a complete point-vibration has elapsed from the moment shown in (1). The wave A has here moved forward into the position indicated by the dotted lines.

The following rows (3,) (4), (5), &c., show the state of things when two-eighths, three-eighths, four-eighths, &c., of a vibration-period has elapsed since (1). In each, the wave A moves forward one step further.

In (9), a whole vibration-period has elapsed since (1). Accordingly every oscillating point has performed one complete vibration, and returned to the position it held in (1). The wave A, meanwhile, has travelled constantly forward so as to be, in (9), where B was in (1), i.e. to have advanced by one whole wave-length. *The proposition proved for waves due to transverse vibrations in § 8 is thus* shown to hold good likewise for waves due to longitudinal vibrations.

16. In the waves shown in Fig. 14, the points in the bracket *a* are mutually equidistant, as are also those in the bracket *b*. This is due to the fact that, in the case there represented, the oscillating points move uniformly, i. e. with equal velocity, throughout their paths. If we take other modes of vibration, we shall find that this equidistance no longer exists. Fig. 15 shows three distinct modes of vibration with the wave resulting from each, on the plan of (1) Fig. 14. The extent of vibration, and length of wave, are the same in the three cases.

In (I) the points move quickest at the middle and slowest at the ends, of their paths; in (II) fastest at the ends, and slowest in the middle; in (III) slowest at the left end, and fastest at the right.

The shortest distance separating any two points contained in *a* is, in (I), that between 7 and 8; in (II), that between 8 and 9; in (III), that between 5 and 6. The corresponding greatest distances are, in (I), between 2 and 3; in (II), between 1 and 2; in (III), between 4 and 5. The remaining points likewise exhibit differences of relative distance in the three cases. Thus, the positions of greatest shortening, and greatest lengthening, occupy different situations in the wave, and the interme-

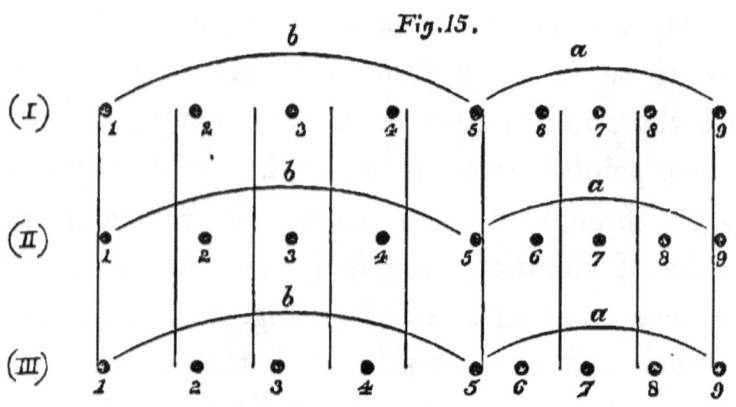

Fig. 15.

diate variations between them proceed according to different laws, when the modes of point-vibration are different. The more points we lay down in their proper positions in a and b, the less abrupt will be the changes of distance between successive points. By indefinitely increasing the number of vibrating points, we should ultimately arrive at a state of things in which perfectly continuous changes of shortening and lengthening intervened between the positions of maximum shortening and maximum lengthening in the same wave.

17. Let us now replace our row of indefinitely numerous points by the slenderest filament of some material whose parts (like those of an elastic string) admit of being compressed, or dilated, at pleasure.

When any portion of the filament is shortened, a larger quantity of material is forced into the space which was before occupied by a smaller quantity. The matter within this space is, therefore, more tightly packed, more *dense*, than it was, i.e. a process of *condensation* has occurred. On the other hand, when a portion of the filament is lengthened, a smaller quantity is made to occupy the space before occupied by a larger quantity. Here the matter is more loosely packed, more *rare*, than it was, i.e. a process of *rarefaction* has taken place.

Let us now suppose the particles, or smallest conceivable atoms, of the filament, to be thrown into successive vibrations in the manner already so fully explained. Alternate states of condensation and rarefaction will then travel along the filament. It will be convenient to call these states 'pulses'— of condensation or rarefaction as the case may be. A pulse of condensation and a pulse of rarefaction together make up a complete wave.

18. The degree of condensation, or rarefaction, existing at any given point of a wave has been shown to depend on the mode in which the particles of the filament vibrate. It is therefore desirable to have some simple method, appealing directly to the eye, of exhibiting the law of any assigned mode of vibration which takes place in a straight line.

We may arrive at such a method by the following considerations.

When a line of particles vibrate longitudinally, they give rise to waves of condensation and rarefaction; when transversely, to waves of displacement on opposite sides of the line of particles in their positions of rest. Nevertheless, if the vibrations in the two cases are identical in all other respects save direction alone, the distance which, at any moment, separates an assigned particle from its position of rest will be the same, whether the vibrations are longitudinal or transverse. It is therefore only necessary to construct the wave corresponding to any system of *transverse* vibrations, in the way shown in § 12, to obtain the means of fixing the position of

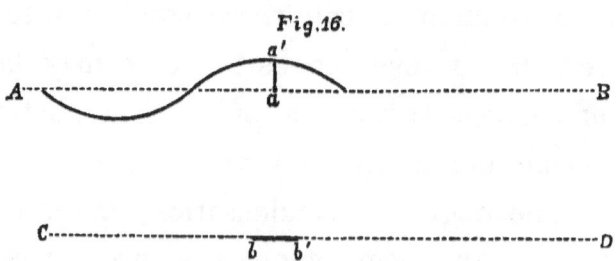

Fig. 16.

an assigned particle, at any given moment, for the same system of vibrations executed longitudinally.

Let AB and CD, Fig. 16, be lines of particles executing vibrations transverse to AB, and along CD, respectively. Let a and b be corresponding particles in their positions of rest. Draw the transverse wave for any given instant of time: the particle originally at a will now be at a', and that originally at b, at b', making bb' equal to aa'.

By performing the same process for different instants, we can find as many corresponding positions of the longitudinally vibrating particle as we please. It is true that we learn nothing *new* by this, since we cannot construct the wave-curve without knowing beforehand the mode of the particle's vibration [§ 12]. Still when we are dealing with longitudinal particle-vibrations, and require to know the law of the variation of condensation and rarefaction at different points of a single wave, it is convenient to have a picture of the mode of vibration by which, as we know [§ 16], that law is determined. Such a picture we have in the form of the wave produced by the same mode of vibration when executed transversely. Let us call the wave so related to a given wave of condensation and rarefaction, its *associated wave*.

19. Before leaving this portion of the subject, it will be advisable to draw the associated wave for that particular mode of longitudinal vibration in which each particle moves as if it were the extremity of a pendulum traversing a path which is very short

compared to the pendulum's length. The meaning of this limitation will be easily seen from Fig. 17.

Let O be the fixed point of suspension; OA the pendulum in its vertical position; AB a portion of a circle with centre O and radius OA; a, b, c, d, points on this circle; AD a horizontal straight line

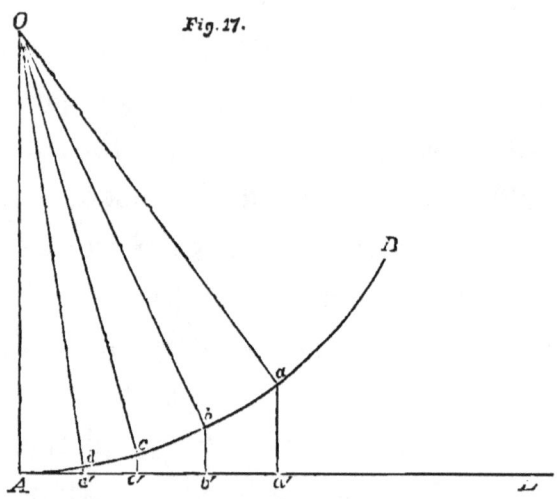

Fig. 17.

through A; aa', bb', cc', dd' verticals through a, b, c, d, respectively. If the pendulum is placed in the position Oa, and left to itself, it will swing through twice the angle aOA before it turns back again. Similarly if started at Ob, it will swing through twice the angle bOA; if at Oc, through twice the angle cOA, and so on. Now, the extremity of the pendulum, when at a, is further from the horizontal line, AD, than when it is at b, since aa' is greater than bb', and at b further than at c. If we make the pendulum vibrate through only a small angle, by starting it, say, in the position Od, its extremity will, throughout its motion, be very near to the horizontal straight line AD. If we make the angle small enough, or, which is the same thing, take Ad sufficiently small compared with OA, we may, without any perceptible error, suppose the end of the pendulum to move in a horizontal straight line, instead of in a circular arc, i. e. along $d'A$ instead of dA. To take an actual case, let us suppose the pendulum to be 10 ft. long, and that its extent of swing is 1 inch on either side of its vertical position. A very easy geometrical calculation will show that the end of the pendulum will never be as much as $\frac{1}{200}$ th of an inch out of the horizontal straight line drawn through it in its lowest position. This is a vanishing quantity; we may, therefore, safely regard the vibration as performed along $d'A$ instead of dA. Such a vibration, though executed in a straight line instead of in the arc of a circle, we may properly call a *pendulum-vibration*, as expressing the law according to which it takes place. This law admits of easy geometrical illustration as follows. Let a ball, or other small object, be attached to some part of an upright wheel revolving uniformly about a fixed axis, so that the ball goes round and round in the same vertical circle with constant velocity. If the sun is in the zenith, i. e. in such a position that the shadows of all objects are thrown vertically, *the shadow of the ball on any horizontal plane below it will move exactly as does the bob of a pendulum.*

The form of the associated wave for longitudinal pendulum-vibrations is shown in Fig. 17 (*a*).

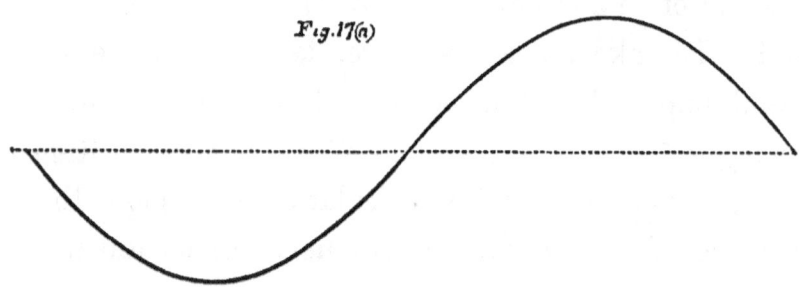

Retaining the *form* of the curve, we may make its amplitude and wave-length as large or as small as we please, as in the case of the waves in Fig. 4, (1) and (2), p. 13.

20. We have examined the transmission of waves due to longitudinal vibrations along a single very slender filament. Suppose that a great number of such filaments are placed side by side in contact with each other, so as to form a uniform material column. If, now, precisely equal waves are transmitted along all the constituent filaments simulta-

neously, successive pulses of condensation and rarefaction will pass along the column. The parts in any assigned transverse section of the column will, obviously, at any given moment of time, all have exactly the same degree of compression or dilatation. When a pulse of condensation is traversing the section, its parts will be more dense, when a pulse of rarefaction is traversing it, less dense, than they would be, were the column transmitting no waves at all, and its separate particles, therefore, absolutely at rest. Let the column with which we have been dealing be the portion of atmospheric air enclosed within a tube of uniform bore. The phenomena just described will then be exactly those which accompany the passage of a sound from one end of the tube to the other. It remains to examine the mechanical cause to which these phenomena are due.

Atmospheric air, in its ordinary condition, exerts a certain pressure on all objects in contact with it. This pressure is adequate to support a vertical column of mercury 30 inches high, as we know by the common barometer. In Fig. 18 is shown a section of a tube closed at one end, with a moveable piston fitting into the other. In (1) the air on both sides of the piston is in the ordinary atmospheric condition, so that the pressure on the right face of the piston is counteracted by an exactly equal and opposite pressure on its left face.

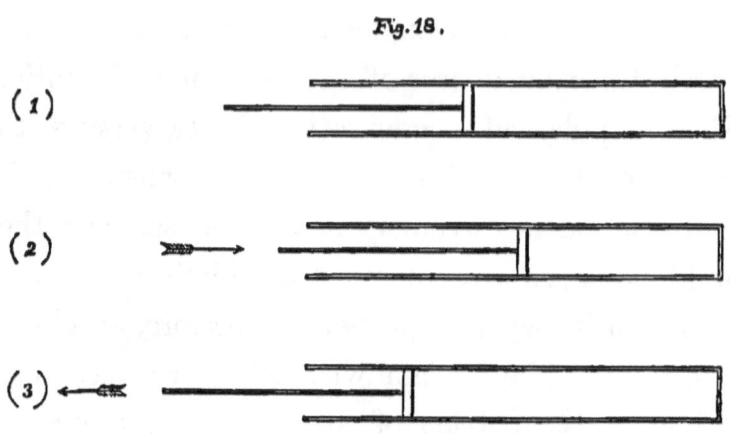

Fig. 18.

In (2) the piston has been moved inwards, so as to compress the air on the right of it. That on its left, being in free communication with the external air, is not permanently affected by the motion of the piston. In order to retain the piston in its forward position, it is necessary to *exert a force upon it*, in the direction of the arrow. If this force is relaxed, the piston is driven back. Since the pressure of the air on the left of the piston is just what it was before, that on its right must necessarily have increased. But this increase of pressure is accompanied by an increase of density, due to the compression of the air on the right of the piston. Hence *increase of pressure accompanies increase of density.*

If, as in (3), we reverse the process, by moving the piston outwards, the extraneous force must be exerted in the opposite direction, as shown by the arrow. The pressure on the right of the piston is therefore less than the normal atmospheric pressure on its left, i. e. *diminution of pressure accompanies diminution of density*. By experiments such as the above, it was shown, by the French philosopher Mariotte, that the pressure of air *varies as its density*.

21. Next, let us take a cylindrical tube open at one end and having a moveable piston fitting into the other, as in Fig. 19.

In (1) the piston is at rest at A, and the air in its ordinary atmospheric condition of density and

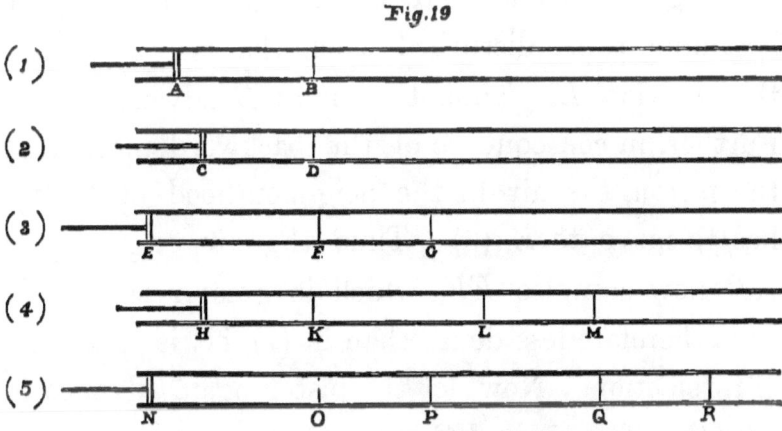

Fig.19

pressure. In (2) the piston is pushed inwards as far as C. While it is moving up to this position, the air-particles in front of it are thrown into motion. Suppose that, at the moment when the piston reaches C, the particles at D are just beginning to be disturbed. The air which, in (1), occupied AB, is now crowded into CD, and is, therefore, denser than that further on in the tube. Now, let the piston be drawn back to E, (3), as much to the left of its original position, A, (1), as, in (2), it was to the right of it. The air in CD, (2), will, while this is taking place, expand into EF; for, being denser, it will also be at a greater pressure, than the air to the right of it. It will, therefore, act on the air in advance of it in the same way as the piston did on the air in contact with it when moving from A, (1) to C, (2). Hence the air in FG will be condensed, G being the point where the air particles are just beginning to be disturbed when the piston reaches the position E. Thus the air at D advances to F. Further, in consequence of the backward motion of the piston, the air in the neighbourhood of C, (2), has to move to E, (3). Thus the air originally in AB now occupies EF, which is greater than AB. It is therefore less dense than in (1), i.e. is in a state of rarefaction. Now, let the piston again advance to H, (4). The air in FG being at a greater pressure than that in its front, and still more so than that in its rear, will expand in both directions, causing a new condensation, LM, to be formed further on, and itself becoming the rarefaction KL, co-operating, at the same time, with the advancing piston to produce in its own rear the condensation HK. In (5) the piston is again where it was in (3). HK has expanded into the rarefaction NO, KL contracted into the condensation OP, LM expanded into the rarefaction PQ, and a new condensation, QR, been formed in front.

The figure makes it clear that each forward stroke of the piston produces a pulse of condensation, and each backward stroke a pulse of rarefaction; but that, when once formed, these pulses travel onwards independently of any external force. They do so, as we have seen, in virtue of the relation which connects the pressure of the air with its density, in other words, on the *elasticity* of the air.

If we suppose our moveable piston withdrawn from the tube, and a vibrating tuning-fork held with the extremity of one prong close to the orifice of the tube, the conditions of the problem will not be essentially modified. Each outward swing of the prong will give rise to a condensed, and each inward swing to a rarefied pulse, and thus, during every complete vibration of the fork, one sonorous wave, consisting of a pulse of condensation and a pulse of rarefaction, will be started on its journey along the tube.

22. We have examined the transmission of Sound along a column of air contained in a tube of uniform bore. A more important case is that in which a sound, originated at an assigned point, spreads out from it freely in all directions. Here we must conceive a series of spherical shells, alternately of condensed and of rarefied air, one inside the other, and all having the point of origination of the sound as their common centre. All the shells must be supposed to expand uniformly like an elastic globular balloon constantly inflated with more and more gas. The great difference between this case and that last considered lies in this, that, as the spherical shells of condensation and rarefaction spread, it is necessary, in order to keep up the wave-motion, to throw larger and larger surfaces of air into vibration; whereas within the tube the transverse section remained the same throughout. Hence, as the same amount of original disturbing force has to set a constantly increasing number of air-particles into motion, it can only do so by proportionately shortening the distances through which the individual particles move, i.e. by diminishing their extent of vibration. Accordingly when Sound-waves spread out freely in all directions, the further any given air-particle is from the point at which the sound originated, the smaller will be the extent of the

vibration into which it will be thrown when the waves reach it.

23. Sounds are either *musical* or *non-musical*. The vast majority of those ordinarily heard—the roaring of the wind, the din of traffic in a crowded thoroughfare—belong to the second class. Musical sounds are, for the most part, to be heard only from instruments constructed to produce them. The difference between the sensations caused in our ears by these two classes of sounds is extremely well marked, and its nature admits of easy analysis. Let a note be struck and held down on the harmonium, or on any instrument capable of producing a sustained tone. However attentively we may listen, we perceive no change or variation in the sound we hear. A perfectly continuous and uniform sensation is experienced as long as the note is held down. If, instead of the harmonium, we employ the pianoforte, where the sound is loudest directly after the moment of percussion, and then gradually dies away, the result of the experiment is that the diminution of loudness is the only change which occurs: the effect produced is the same as if our harmonium had, while sounding out its note, been carried gradually further and further away from us.

In the case of non-musical sounds, variations of a different kind can be easily detected. In the howling of the wind the sound rises to a considerable degree of shrillness, then falls, then rises again, and so on. On parts of the coast, where a shingly beach of considerable extent slopes down to the sea, a sound is heard in stormy weather which varies from the deep thundering roar of the great breakers, to the shrill tearing scream of the shingle dragged along by the retreating surf. Similar variations may be noticed in sounds of small intensity, such as the rustling of leaves, the chirping of insects, and the like. The difference, then, between musical and non-musical sounds seems to lie in this, that the former are constant, while the latter are continually varying. The human voice can produce sounds of both classes. In singing a sustained note it remains quite steady, neither rising nor falling. Its conversational tone, on the other hand, is perpetually varying in height even within a single syllable; directly it ceases so to vary, its non-musical character disappears, and it becomes what is commonly called 'sing-song.'

We may then define a musical sound as a *steady* sound, a non-musical sound as an *unsteady* sound. It is true we may often be puzzled to say whether a particular sound is musical or not: this arises, however, from no defect in our definition, but from the fact that such sounds consist of two elements, a musical and a non-musical, of which the latter may be the more powerful, and therefore absorb our attention, until it is specially directed to the former. For instance, a beginner on the violin often produces a sound in which the irregular scratching of the bow predominates over the regular tone of the string. In bad flute playing, an unsteady hissing sound accompanies the naturally sweet tone of the instrument, and may easily surpass it in intensity. In the tones of the more imperfect musical instruments, such as drums and cymbals, the non-musical element is very prominent, while in such sounds as the hammering of metals, or the roar of a water-fall, we may be able to recognize only a *trace* of the musical element, all but extinguished by its boisterous companion.

We have seen that Sound reaches our ears by means of rapid vibrations of the particles of the atmosphere. It has also been shown that *steadiness* is the characteristic feature of musical, as distinguished from non-musical, sounds. We may infer hence that the motion of the air corresponding to a single musical sound will be itself steady, i.e. that *equal numbers of equal vibrations will be executed in precisely equal times.* This conception of the physical conditions under which musical sounds are produced will suffice for the present. We proceed to consider in detail the various ways in which such sounds may differ from each other, and to investigate the mechanical cause to which each such difference is to be referred. In what follows, by the word 'sound' will always be meant 'musical sound,' unless the contrary be expressly stated.

CHAPTER II.

ON LOUDNESS AND PITCH.

24. A musical sound may vary in three different respects. Let a note be played, first by a single violin, then, by two, by three, and so on, until we have all the violins of an orchestra in unison upon it. This is a variation of *loudness* only. Next, let a succession of notes be played on any instrument of uniform power, such as the harmonium without the expression-stop, or on the principal manual of an organ, only one combination of stops being in either case used. Here we have a variation of *pitch* alone. Lastly, let one and the same note be successively struck on a number of pianofortes of the same size, but by different makers. The sounds heard will all have exactly the same pitch, and *about* the same degree of loudness; nevertheless they will exhibit decided differences of character. The tone of one instrument will be rich and full, of another ringing and metallic, that of a third will be described as 'wiry,' of a fourth as 'tinkling,' and so on.

Sounds thus related to each other are said to vary in *quality* only. The instances just considered have the advantage of simplicity, since they allow of changes in loudness, pitch, and quality being exhibited separately. They are, however, less striking than other cases where sounds vary in two, or in all three, of these respects at the same time. A practised ear may be requisite to detect the difference between the tone of two pianofortes, but no one is in danger of mistaking, for instance, a flute for a trumpet. There is here, no doubt, considerable difference of loudness as well as of quality, but let the more powerful instrument be placed at such a distance that it sounds no louder than the weaker one, and the distinction between the two kinds of *tone* will be still quite decisive.

Two assigned musical sounds thus may differ from each other in loudness *or* pitch *or* quality, and agree in the other two—or they may differ in any two of these, and agree in the third—or they may differ in all three. There is, however, no *other* respect in which they *can* differ, and accordingly we know all about a musical sound as soon as we know its loudness, its pitch, and its quality. These three elements *determine* the sound, just as the lengths of the three sides of a triangle determine the triangle.

25. The loudness of a musical sound depends entirely, as we shall easily see, on the extent of oscillatory movement performed by the individual

particles composing the medium through which the sound is conveyed to our ears. A sound-producing instrument can be readily observed to be in a state of rapid vibratory motion. The vibrations of a tuning-fork are perceptible to the eye in the fuzzy, half-transparent, rim which surrounds its prongs when it is struck; and to the touch, if, after striking the fork, we place a finger gently against one of the prongs. The harder we hit the fork the louder is its sound, and the larger, estimated by both the above modes of observation, are its vibrations. The experiment may be tried equally well on any pianoforte whose construction allows the wires to be uncovered. It is natural to infer that a vibration on the part of a sound-producing instrument communicates to the particles of the air in contact with it a corresponding movement. Thus a sound of given loudness is conveyed by vibrations of given extent, and, if the sound increases or diminishes in intensity, the extent of the vibrations will increase or diminish with it.

We conclude, then, that the loudness of a musical sound depends solely on the extent of excursion of the particles which constitute the conveying medium *in the neighbourhood of our ears*. This last condition is clearly essential, since a sound grows more and more feeble, the greater our distance from the point where it is produced. This diminution of intensity with the increase of distance from the origin of sound is a direct consequence of the connection between loudness and extent of vibration. We have seen [§ 22] that the further an air particle is from the point where a sound is produced, the smaller will be the extent of the vibration into which it is thrown by the sonorous wave. Hence, as the sound advances, it will necessarily become feebler, provided always that the waves are permitted to spread out in all directions. If they are confined, say, in a tube, the intensity of the sound will not diminish with anything like the same rapidity. We have here the theory of message-pipes, which are used in large establishments to enable a conversation to be carried on between distant parts of a building. A whisper, inaudible to a person close to the speaker, may, by their means, be perfectly well heard by a listener at the other end of the tube.

26. We have next to enquire to what mechanical causes differences in the *pitch* of musical sounds are to be referred. Rough observation at once indicates the direction in which we must look. If we draw the point of a pencil along a rough surface, first slowly and then more quickly, the sound heard will be distinctly shriller the more rapid the movement of the pencil. As its point passes over the

minute elevations and depressions which constitute the roughness of the surface, a series of irregular vibrations are set up in the materials of the surface, and by them communicated to the air. The more rapid are these vibrations, the shriller does the sound become. The instrument described below, which is called a 'Syren,' gives us the means of following up with accuracy the hint just obtained.

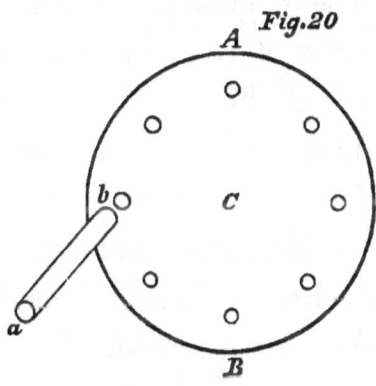

AB is a thin circular disc of tin or card-board, which, by means of a multiplying wheel, can be set in rapid revolution about a fixed axis through its centre, C. A series of holes (eight in the figure) are punched in the disc at equal distances along a circle having its centre at C. A small tube, ab, is held with one end close to one of the holes. If, while the disc is rotating, we blow steadily and continuously into the tube at a, a certain quantity of air will pass through the disc whenever a hole traverses the orifice b, of the tube ab. During the intervals of time which elapse between the passage of adjacent holes across b, *no* air can pass through the disc. Hence, if the disc be revolving uniformly, a series of such discharges will succeed each other at perfectly regular intervals of time. The air on the other side of the disc will necessarily be agitated by the process. Every time that air is driven through one of the holes, an increase of pressure occurs close to it, and accordingly a pulse of condensation is formed there. The elastic force of the air will give rise to a pulse of rarefaction during each interval between successive discharges. Hence the Syren supplies us with a regular series of alternate condensations and rarefactions which when sufficiently rapid will, as we have seen, produce a musical sound.

27. While air is being blown steadily into the tube, let the disc be made to revolve slowly, and then with gradually increasing rapidity. At first nothing will be audible but a series of faint intermittent throbs, due to the impact of the air driven through the tube against the successive portions of the disc which separate its holes. This sound may be exactly reproduced by moving the fore-finger to and fro rapidly before the lips, while blowing through them. It contributes nothing to the proper musical sound of the instrument, and is only audible in its imme-

diate neighbourhood. Presently, a deep musical sound begins to be heard, which, as the velocity of rotation increases, constantly rises in pitch. The acuteness of the sound thus obtainable depends solely on the speed to which we can urge the instrument, and is therefore limited only by the driving-power at our command. The rise of pitch in this experiment is perfectly *continuous*, that is to say, the sound of the Syren, in passing from a graver to a more acute note, goes through *every possible intermediate degree of pitch*. It is important that we should familiarize ourselves with this conception of the continuity of the scale of pitch, because in the instrument from which our ideas on this subject are usually obtained—the pianoforte—the pitch alters *discontinuously*, i.e. by a series of jumps of half a tone each, and we are thus tempted to ignore the intervening degrees of pitch, or even to suppose them non-existent. The more perfect musical instruments, such as the human voice or the violin, are as capable as the Syren of passing through all degrees of pitch from one note to another in the way called '*portamento*' or '*slurring*.'

It is clear from the nature of the Syren's construction, that the only change which can take place during the rise of pitch is the increased number of impulses communicated to, and therefore of vibrations set up in, the external air, during any given interval of time. If, when a note of given pitch has been attained by the Syren, we check any further increase of velocity, and cause the disc to rotate uniformly at the rate which it has just reached, no further alteration of pitch will occur, and the note will be steadily held by the instrument, so long as the uniform rotation of its disc is kept up. Hence *the number of aerial vibrations executed in a given time determines the pitch of the sound heard.*

28. The Syren, besides teaching us this most important fact, gives us the means of determining the number of vibrations corresponding to any given note. If we know the number of rotations which the disc has performed in a given time, we have only to multiply this number by the number of holes on the disc in order to ascertain how many tube-discharges have occurred, and therefore how many corresponding aerial vibrations have been performed, in the period in question. The Syren is provided with a counting-apparatus which registers the number of times its disc rotates per second.

In order, therefore, to obtain the number of vibrations in a second which correspond to an assigned note, we have only to proceed as follows. Let the note be steadily sounded by some instrument of sustained power, e.g. organ or harmonium, and then cause the Syren sound to mount the scale until its pitch coincides with that of the note under examination. At the instant of coincidence read the figure indicated by the counting-apparatus. This, multiplied by the number of holes in the disc, gives the number of vibrations per second required. It will be convenient, for the sake of shortness, to call the number of vibrations per second, to which any note is due, the *vibration-number* of the note in question. It is clear, from what has gone before, that any assigned degree of pitch can be permanently registered, when once its vibration-number has been ascertained.

29. The Syren shows that, below a certain rate of vibration, no musical sounds are produced. The position of the absolute limit thus placed to the gravity of such sounds cannot be exactly defined, and probably varies somewhat for different ears. The lowest note on the largest modern organs has $16\frac{1}{2}$ for its vibration-number, but it is a moot question whether the musical character of this note can be recognized or not.

In any case we may regard the lower limit of musical sounds as situated in the immediate neighbourhood of this degree of pitch. For some distance above the limit the musical character continues very imperfect, and it is not until we reach $41\frac{1}{4}$ vibrations per second, the lowest note of the double-bass, that we get a satisfactory musical sound. There is no corresponding limit absolutely barring the scale of pitch in the opposite direction, but sounds above a certain degree of acuteness become painful to the ear, and therefore unfit for musical purposes. The highest note of the piccolo, the shrillest sound heard in the orchestra, makes 4752 vibrations per second. And this we may regard as constituting a practical superior limit to the scale of pitch at the disposal of musical art. The extremest range attainable by exceptional human voices, from the deepest note of a bass to the highest of a soprano, lies, roughly speaking, between 50 and 1500 vibrations per second. Ordinary chorus voices range from 100 to 900, or 1000 vibrations per second. The number of sounds within the limits of the musical scale, which can be recognized as possessing distinct degrees of pitch, will vary with the acuteness of perception of individual observers. Trained violinists are said to be able to distinguish about seven hundred sounds in a single octave, which would give nearly five thousand for the whole scale. But, since the difficulty of fixing the pitch with accuracy increases very rapidly with very low or very high sounds, this estimate would probably much exceed the limits of what could be achieved by the very finest ear. We shall, however, be well within the mark if we assume that an ordinary ear can recognize, on the average, between one and two hundred sounds in an octave, or fully one thousand in the whole scale. There is nothing in the continuously shading-off gradations of pitch to indicate what sounds should be picked out to form agreeable sequences, or combinations, with each other. Nevertheless the human mind, working on this seeming chaos from the earliest dawn of musical art, has reduced it to order by discovering the following principle.

30. When one sound has been arbitrarily selected as the starting-point, there are a certain number of other sounds, having fixed relations of pitch to that previously chosen, which are capable of forming, with it and with each other, melodic and harmonic effects especially pleasing to the ear. These are the notes of the ordinary major and minor scales, the original sound of reference being the common *tonic*, or *keynote*, of those scales. In saying that these sounds have fixed mutual relations of pitch, we merely state formally an obvious fact. A familiar melody is recognized equally well whether heard in the deep tones of a man's, or in the shrill notes of a child's voice. Whether the singer pitches it on a low or on a high note of his voice makes no difference in the melody itself. In fact the correctness with which an

air is sung no more depends on the exact pitch of the note on which the singer starts it, than does the faithfulness of a plan on the precise *scale* which the draughtsman has adopted. It is sufficient that the constituent notes of the melody should have fixed *mutual relations* of pitch, just as, in the plan, the several objects represented need only be drawn *in proportion* to their actual dimensions.

The difference in pitch of any two notes is called the *interval* between them: it is on accuracy of intervals that music essentially depends.

31. The most important interval in the scale is the *octave*. It is that which separates the highest note of a peal of eight bells from the lowest. When a bass and a treble voice sing the same melody together, the notes of the latter are usually one octave above those of the former. The octave has this peculiarity, shared by no other interval, that, if starting from any note we choose, we ascend to that an octave above it, then to that an octave above the last, and so on, we get a number of notes which sound perfectly smooth and agreeable when heard all together. The same thing holds good, if we descend by a succession of octaves from the note fixed on as our starting-point. Hence we may conveniently regard the whole scale of pitch as divided into a series of octaves, taken upwards and downwards from

some one sound arbitrarily selected. Narrower intervals situated in any one octave are repeated in all the other octaves, so that, when we have settled those intervals for *a single octave*, we have settled them for all the rest. Within the limits of each octave, the common major scale presents us with *seven notes*, or, if we include that which forms the starting point of the next octave, with *eight*. The fact that the eighth note is the octave of the first explains the meaning of the word 'octave,' i.e. 'eighth' (*Latin:* '*octavus*').

The eight notes are those of an ordinary peal of the same number of bells, or of the white keys of the pianoforte between two adjacent C's. We may, for convenience of reference, number them 1, 2, 3......8, beginning with the lowest note, or tonic. The following nomenclature is used to describe the intervals formed by the several notes *with the tonic*.

Notes forming interval.	Name of interval.
1 and 2	Second
1 3	Major Third
1 4	Fourth
1 5	Fifth
1 6	Major Sixth
1 7	Major Seventh
1 8	Eighth or Octave.

When two notes of the same pitch are sounded together, e.g. by two instruments, or by two voices, the notes are said to be in *unison*. Though there is here no difference of pitch whatever, it is convenient to rank the unison as an interval. With this explanation we may add to the above table that 1 and 1 form the interval of an unison. The reader must carefully avoid giving to the 'Thirds,' 'Fourths,' &c., which he meets with in music the meanings attached to the same words in fractional arithmetic, with which they have absolutely nothing to do. A 'Fifth,' for example, does not stand for a *fifth part* of an octave, or indeed for a *fifth part* of anything, but for the difference of pitch between the first and fifth notes of the scale.

The several pairs of notes forming the intervals laid down in our table do not all produce smooth and agreeable effects when sounded together. The following pairs blend pleasantly:

$$1—3,\ 1—4,\ 1—5,\ 1—6,\ 1—8;$$

the remaining two,

$$1—2\ \text{and}\ 1—7,$$

give rise to decidedly harsh effects. The intervals in the first line are therefore classed as *concords*, those in the second as *discords*.

32. The minor scale has the notes 1, 2, 4, 5, 8 in common with the major scale. It substitutes for 3

a sound lying between that note and 2, which forms with 1 a consonant interval called the Minor Third. According to circumstances it may either retain 6, or replace it by a sound lying between that note and 5, which makes with 1 a concord called the Minor Sixth. Similarly it may employ 7, or, in the room of that note, a fresh sound situated below it, but above 6, which with 1 forms a discord called the Minor Seventh.

Thus, including the octave, the two scales together give us a series of eleven notes, which, severally combined with the tonic, form ten distinct intervals. They are expressed in musical notation as follows:—

The reader should endeavour to familiarize himself with these intervals, so that, when he hears the pair of notes which form any one of them successively sounded, he may at once be able to name the interval.

33. The Syren enables us to obtain simple numerical measures of the intervals exhibited on this page.

Let a second circular row, containing sixteen holes, be punched in its disc, and the instrument set uniformly rotating. If we now blow alternately against the 8-hole row, and the 16-hole row, we shall find that the sound produced at the latter is precisely one octave higher in pitch than the sound produced at the former. If we increase or diminish the velocity of rotation, both sounds will, of course, rise or fall proportionately, but the interval between them will remain unaffected and equal as before, to an exact octave. The number of air-discharges corresponding to the more acute sound is, in this case, evidently twice as large, in any given time, as the number, during the same time, for the graver sound. Accordingly we have the following result.

When two sounds differ by a single octave, the higher sound makes exactly twice as many vibrations in any assigned time as the lower.

Next let a row of 12 holes be punched in the disc of the Syren. Taking this row with the 8-hole row, and proceeding as in the last instance, we find that the more acute sound forms a Fifth with the graver one. The numbers of discharges in any given time are here as 12 to 8, i.e. as 3 to 2. The result therefore is as follows: *when two sounds differ by a Fifth, the higher sound makes exactly three vibrations during the time in which the lower sound makes two.*

If we take the 16-hole and 12-hole rows together, the interval amounts to a Fourth; accordingly, *when two sounds differ by a Fourth, the higher sound makes exactly four vibrations during the time in which the lower sound makes three.*

34. The results just obtained may be somewhat more concisely stated. During *one second of time*, the upper of two sounds differing by an octave makes a number of vibrations, which is to the number made by the lower sound as 2 to 1. For a Fifth the ratio is as 3 to 2. For a Fourth it is as 4 to 3. Remembering, then, the definition of the vibration-number of an assigned sound [§ 28], we may express our three results as follows:—

When two sounds form with each other the intervals of an octave, a Fifth or a Fourth, their vibration-numbers are to each other, in the first case as 2 to 1, in the second as 3 to 2, in the third as 4 to 3.

A ratio is most easily expressed by a fraction. Thus we may regard the fraction $\frac{3}{2}$ as denoting the interval of a Fifth. It may be taken as an abbreviated statement of the fact that, when two sounds form a Fifth with each other, the more acute makes 3 vibrations while the graver makes 2.

35. By suitable experiments, similar numerical relations to those already established may be ob-

tained for all the intervals already considered. A fraction can thus be determined for each interval, in the manner exemplified in the case of the Fifth. We will call this fraction the *vibration-fraction* of the interval in question. The accompanying table gives, in the second column, the vibration-fractions corresponding to the intervals named in the first; and in the third, describes the consonant or dissonant character of the intervals.

Name of interval.	Vibration-fraction.	Character of interval.
Unison	$\frac{1}{1}$	concord
Second	$\frac{9}{8}$	discord
Minor Third	$\frac{6}{5}$	concord
Major Third	$\frac{5}{4}$	concord
Fourth	$\frac{4}{3}$	concord
Fifth	$\frac{3}{2}$	concord
Minor Sixth	$\frac{8}{5}$	concord
Major Sixth	$\frac{5}{3}$	concord
Minor Seventh	$\frac{16}{9}$	discord
Major Seventh	$\frac{15}{8}$	discord
Octave	$\frac{2}{1}$	concord

It is noticeable that the dissonant intervals involve higher numbers in their vibration-fractions than the consonant intervals do; the latter, with the solitary exception of the Minor Sixth, having nothing beyond 6, while the former bring in 9, 15 and 16.

36. By the help of the last table, we can calculate the vibration-numbers of all the notes within a single octave which belong to the major or minor keys *as soon as the vibration-number of the tonic is given.* For instance, let middle C of the pianoforte (vib.-no. 264) be the tonic. From the second line of the table, we see that the vibration-number of D must be to 264 in the ratio of 9 to 8. It must therefore be equal to $\frac{9}{8} \times 264$, or 297. For E♭, by exactly similar reasoning, we obtain $\frac{6}{5} \times 264$ or $316\frac{4}{5}$; for E, $\frac{5}{4} \times 264$, or 330.

The student should work out the remaining cases for himself.

The complete results for the major scale are as follow:—

In order to extend the scale another octave upwards, we have only to multiply each vibration-number by 2. A second multiplication by 2 will raise it by another octave, and so on. Conversely, in order to pass to the octave below, we divide each vibration-number by 2. To descend a second octave we repeat the operation, and so on.

Thus the pitch of the tonic absolutely fixes the pitch of *every note*, in the scale of which it is the starting-point.

Before we proceed to investigate the mechanical equivalent of the third element [§ 24] of a musical sound, its quality, it will be convenient briefly to examine a subject possessing an important bearing on that enquiry. This we shall do in the next chapter.

CHAPTER III.

ON RESONANCE.

37. When a sounding body causes another body to emit sound, we have an instance of a very remarkable phenomenon called *resonance*. The German term for it, 'co-vibration' (*Mitschwingung*), possesses the merit of at once indicating its essential meaning, namely, the setting up of vibrations in an instrument, not by a blow or other immediate action upon it, but indirectly as the result of the vibrations of another instrument. In order to produce the effect, we have only to press down very gently one of the keys of a pianoforte, so as to raise the damper, without making any sound, and then sing loudly, into the instrument, the corresponding note. When the voice ceases, the instrument will continue to sustain the note, which will then gradually fade away. If the key is allowed to rise again before the sound is extinct, it will abruptly cease. A similar experiment may be tried, as follows, on any horizontal pianoforte which allows the wires to be uncovered. Each note is, it is well

known, produced by two, or by three, wires. Having, as in the previous case, raised one of the dampers without striking the note, twitch *one* of the corresponding wires sharply with the finger-nail, and then wait a few seconds. The vibrations will, in this interval, have communicated themselves to the other string, or strings, belonging to the note pressed down: if, now, the first wire be stopped by applying the tip of the finger to the point where it was at first twitched, the same note, produced by these transmitted vibrations, will continue to be sustained by the remaining wire or wires.

A more instructive method of studying resonance is to take two unison tuning-forks, strike one of them, and hold it near the other, but without touching it. The second fork will then commence sounding by resonance, and will continue to produce its note though the first fork be brought to silence. It is essential to the success of this experiment that the two forks should be rigorously in unison. If the pitch of one of them be lowered by causing a small pellet of wax to adhere to the end of one of its prongs, the effect of resonance will no longer be produced, even though the alteration of pitch be too small to be recognized by the ear. Further, the phenomenon requires a certain appreciable length of time to develope itself; for, if the silent fork be only *momentarily* exposed to the influence of its vocal fellow, no result ensues. The resonance, when produced, is at first extremely feeble, and gradually increases in intensity under the continued action of the originally-excited fork. Some seconds must elapse before the maximum-resonance is attained. The conditions of our experiment show, directly, that the resonance of the second fork was due to the transmission, *by the air*, of the vibrations of the first, the successive air-impulses falling in such a manner on the fork as to produce a *cumulative effect*. If we bear in mind the disproportionate mass of the body set in motion compared to that of the air acting upon it,—steel being more than six thousand times as heavy as atmospheric air, for equal bulks,—we cannot fail to regard this as a very surprising fact.

Let us examine the mechanical causes to which it is due. Suppose a heavy weight to be suspended from a fixed support by a flexible string, so as to form a pendulum of the simplest kind. In order to cause it to perform oscillations of considerable extent by the application of a number of small impulses, we proceed as follows. As soon as, by the first impulse, the weight has been set vibrating through a small distance, we take care that every succeeding impulse is impressed *in the direction in which the weight is moving at the time*. Each impulse, thus applied, will cause the pendulum to oscillate through a larger angle than before, and, the effects of many impulses being in this way added together, an extensive swing of the pendulum is the result.

When the distance through which the weight travels to and fro, though in itself considerable, is *small compared to the length of the supporting string*, the time of oscillation is the same for any extent of swing within this limit, and depends only on the length of the string. My readers will find this important principle illustrated in any Manual of Elementary Mechanics, and I must ask them to take it for granted here. For the sake of simplicity, let us suppose that we are dealing with a *second's* pendulum, *i.e.* one of such a length as to perform one complete oscillation in each second, and therefore to make a single forward or backward swing in each half second. It will be clear, from what has been said above, that the most rapid effect will be produced on the motion of the pendulum, by applying a forward and a backward impulse respectively during each alternate half second, or, which is the same thing, administering *a pair of to and fro impulses during each complete oscillation of the pendulum*. We have a simple instance of such a proceeding in the way in which a couple of boys set a heavily laden swing in violent motion. They stand facing each other, and each boy, when the swing is moving away from him, helps it along with a vigorous push.

38. The above considerations enable us to explain how a sounding-fork excites the vibrations of another fork in unison with itself, through the medium of the intervening air. When a continuous musical note is being sounded, we know that, at any one point we choose to fix upon, the air is undergoing a series of rapid changes, becoming alternately denser, and less dense; than it would be were the sound to cease. The increase of density is accompanied by an increase of pressure; its diminution by a diminution of pressure [§ 20].

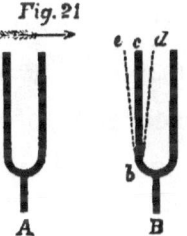

Fig. 21

Let A, Fig. 21, be the sounding-fork, B that whose vibrations are to be excited by resonance, and let us consider the effect of the alternations of pressure on the air at c on the prong bc. The increase of pressure will tend to move the prong into the position bd, its subsequent diminution will facilitate the elastic recoil of the fork, supported also by the superior density of the air on the other side of the prong, and thus tend to bring the prong into the position bc', further to the left of its original position, bc, than bd was to the right of it. Thus the alternate condensations and rarefactions of the Soundwaves impress on the fork B corresponding impulses in opposite directions. One pair of such impulses is applied regularly during each complete vibration of B, since they are due to the vibrations of A, which is in unison with B. Further, for the small extent of vibration with which we have here to deal, the prongs of a tuning-fork move exactly according to the same law as a pendulum[1]. Accordingly, these air-impulses are applied under precisely the conditions which we found to be most favourable to the rapid development of vibratory motion. The large number of such impulses which succeed each other in a few seconds, make up for the feebleness of each by itself. It is in accordance with this, that resonance is produced more slowly between unison-forks of low, than between those of high, pitch. I find that, with two making 256 vibrations per second, about one second is requisite to bring out an audible resonance; while with another pair, making 1920 vibrations per second, I am not able to damp the first fork sufficiently soon after striking it, to prevent the other from making itself heard.

[1] This will be proved in § 70.

39. A column of air is easily set in resonant vibration by a note of suitable pitch. The roughest experiment suffices to establish this fact. We have only to roll up a piece of paper, so as to make a little cylinder six inches long and an inch or two in diameter, with both ends open, and to hold a common C tuning-fork close to one of the apertures, after striking it briskly. As soon as the fork reaches the position (1) Fig. 22, its tone will unmistakeably swell out. In order to estimate the increase of intensity produced, it is a good plan to move the fork rapidly to and fro, a few times, between the positions (1) and (2).

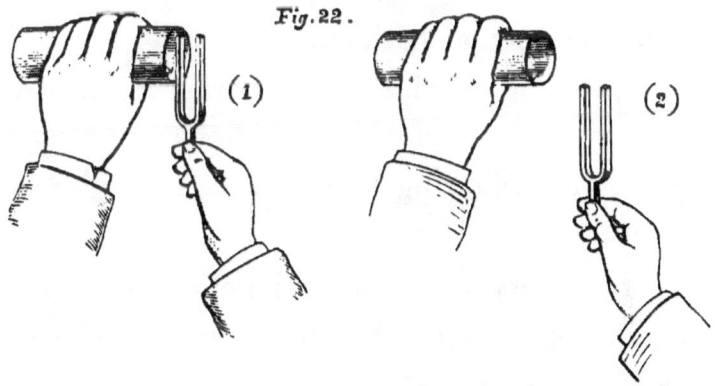

Fig. 22.

In the first case we have the full effect of resonance, in the second only the unassisted tone of the fork, and the contrast is very marked. We may shorten or lengthen our cylinder, within certain limits, and still obtain the phenomena of resonance, but the greatest reinforcement of tone we can attain with the fork selected will be produced by an air-column about six inches long.

If we close one end of the paper cylinder, by placing it, for instance, on a table, and repeat our experiment at the open end, only a very weak resonance is produced; but we obtain a powerful resonance by operating with a fork (♪) making *half as many vibrations per second* as that before employed. In this case, then, a column of air contained in a cylinder, of which one end was closed, resounded powerfully to a note one octave below that which elicited its most vigorous resonance when contained in a cylinder open at both ends.

By operating in this fashion, with forks of different pitch, on air-columns of different lengths, we arrive at the following laws, which are universally true:—

1. For every single musical note there is a corresponding air-column of definite length which resounds the most powerfully to that note.

2. The maximum resonance of air in a closed pipe is produced by a note one octave below that to which an open pipe of the same length resounds the most powerfully.

RESONANT AIR-COLUMNS.

40. In order to ascertain the precise relation between the pitch of a note and the length of the corresponding air-column, we will examine the way in which resonance is produced in a column of air contained in a pipe closed at one end.

Let A, Fig. 23, be the open, and B the closed, ends of the pipe, and let us, for a moment, replace the contained air by an elastic spiral spring fastened at B, and of length equal to AB.

Fig. 23.

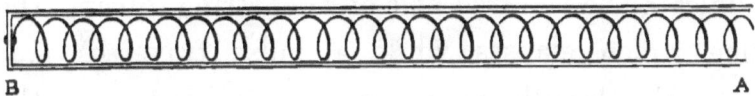

B   A

Suppose the end of the spring suddenly pushed a little way from A towards B. The coils of the spring nearest A will be squeezed together, and this condensed state of the spring will travel along it until it reaches B. The end of the pipe will there cause the condensation to rebound, and travel back again to A. If let alone, the end of the spring would now protrude slightly beyond the open end of the tube, the coils near A would be drawn somewhat apart and a rarefaction would in consequence pass along AB and after reflexion at B return to A, where it would meet the end of the spring just contracting to its original length. The elasticity of the spring would, thus, cause it to lengthen and shorten as a whole, in consequence of the single push originally given it, and this motion would for a time continue, its successive periods being four times the space of time occupied by a pulse of condensation or rarefaction in traversing the length of the tube. The free end of the wire may, however, be pulled and pushed, alternately, so as to reinforce each pulse as it arrives at the open end of the tube, and in this manner the maximum of motion will be communicated to the spring. In this case, one outward, and one inward, impulse of the hand must be communicated to the free end of the string, during the time which elapses while a pulse traverses four times the length of the tube. Reverting to the actual conditions of our problem, we have the resonance of the air-column, in place of the alternate lengthening and shortening of the spring. For the to and fro motion of the hand at A, we must substitute that of the prong of the vibrating fork. The sound-pulse traverses four times the length of the tube while the fork is performing one complete vibration. We know, however [§§ 8 and 15], that, during this latter period, the sound-pulse due to the fork's action traverses precisely one wave-length corresponding to the pitch of the note produced by the fork. Hence, for maximum resonance in the case of a closed pipe, the wave-length corresponding to the note sounded must be four times as great as the length of the air-column, or the length of the column one quarter of the wave-length.

41. These principles give us the explanation of a useful appliance for intensifying the sound of a tuning-fork. Such a fork, when held in the hand after being struck, communicates but little of its vibration to the surrounding air; when, however, its handle is screwed into one side of an empty wooden box of suitable dimensions, in the way shown in Fig. 24, the tone becomes much louder. The vibrations of the fork pass from its handle to the wood of the box,

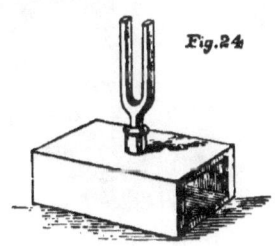

and thence to the air-column within, which is of appropriate length for maximum resonance to the fork's note. This convenient adjunct to a tuning-fork goes by the name of a 'resonance-box.'

42. When a number of musical sounds are going on at once, it is generally difficult, and often impossible, for the unaided ear to decide whether an individual note is, or is not, present in the whole mass of sound heard. If, however, we had an instrument which intensified the tone of the note of

which we were in search, without similarly reinforcing others which there was any risk of our mistaking for it, our power of recognizing the note in question would be proportionately increased. Such an instrument has been invented by Helmholtz. It consists of a hollow ball of brass with two apertures at opposite ends of a diameter, as shown in Fig. 25.

The larger aperture allows the vibrations of the external air to be communicated to that within the ball; the smaller aperture passes through a nipple of convenient form for insertion in the ear of the observer. The air contained in the ball resounds very powerfully to one single note of definite pitch, whence the instrument has been named, by its inventor, a *resonator*. The best way of using it is, first, to stop one ear closely, and then to insert the nipple of the instrument in the other; as often as the resonator's own note is sounded in the external air, the instrument will sing it into the ear of the observer with extraordinary emphasis, and thus at once single out that note from among a crowd of others differing from it in pitch. A series of such resonators, tuned to particular previously selected notes, constitutes an apparatus for analyzing a composite sound into the simple tones of which it is made up.

CHAPTER IV.

ON QUALITY.

43. The laws of resonance enable us to establish a remarkable, and by most persons utterly unsuspected, fact, viz. that the notes of nearly every regular musical instrument with which we are familiar, are not, as they are ordinarily taken to be, single tones of one determinate pitch, but *composite* sounds containing an *assemblage* of such tones. These are always members of a regular series, forming fixed intervals with each other, which may be thus stated: if we number the separate single tones, of which any given sound is made up, 1, 2, 3, &c., beginning with the lowest, and ascending in pitch, we have

- (1) The deepest, or fundamental, tone, which is commonly treated as determining the pitch of the whole sound.
- (2) A tone one octave above (1).
- (3) A tone a Fifth above (2), i.e. a Twelfth above (1).

IV. § 43.] CONSTITUENTS OF COMPOSITE SOUNDS. 83

(4) A tone a Fourth above (3), i.e. two octaves above (1).

(5) A tone a Major Third above (4), i.e. two octaves and a Major Third above (1).

(6) A tone a Minor Third above (5), i.e. two octaves and a Fifth above (1).

These are the most important members of the series. Their vibration-numbers are connected by a simple law, which is easily deduced from the above relations. If the fundamental tone makes 100 vibrations per second, (2) will make twice as many i.e. 200; (3) being a Fifth above (2), will have for its vibration-number, $\frac{3}{2} \times 200$, or 300. For (4), which is a Fourth above (3), we get similarly $\frac{4}{3} \times 300$, or 400; for (5) $\frac{5}{4} \times 400$, or 500; for (6), $\frac{6}{5} \times 500$, or 600. Thus the numbers come out 100, 200, 300 and so on, or, generally, whatever be the vibration-number of (1), those of (2), (3), (4), &c., are respectively *twice*, *three times*, *four times*, *&c.* as great. Subjoined, in musical notation, is the series of tones complete up to the tenth, taking C in the bass clef as our fundamental tone, though any other would do equally well.

6—2

The asterisk denotes that the pitch of the 7th tone is not precisely that of the note by which it is here represented. It is in fact slightly less acute.

The reader must not suppose, that, because the tones into which a note of a musical instrument may usually be decomposed are members of a fixed series, *all* those which we have written down are necessarily present in *every* such note. All that is meant to be asserted is, that those which *are* present, be they few or many, must occupy positions determined by the law connecting each tone with its fundamental. The sound may contain, say, (1), (3), and (5) only, or (1), (4) and (8) only, and so on, the rest being entirely absent, but *in no case can a tone intermediate in pitch between any two consecutive members of the series make its appearance.*

44. Experimental evidence shall now be produced in support of the extremely important proposition just enunciated.

We will begin with the sounds of the pianoforte. Let the note be first silently pressed down, and then [♪] be vigorously struck, and, after three or four seconds, allowed to rise again. The lower note is at once extinguished, but, we now hear its octave sounding with considerable force from the wires of [♪]. If we permit the damper to fall back on these, by releasing the note hitherto held down, the whole sound is immediately cut off.

Next, retaining the same fundamental note, [♪], let [♪] be quietly freed from its damper, and the experiment repeated as before. We shall then hear this note sounding on after the extinction of [♪]. Similar results may be obtained with the three next tones, [♪], but they drop off very rapidly in intensity. The tones above [♪] are so weak as to be practically insensible. The series of tones produced in this succession of trials can only be due to resonance. But, as has been already shown, the vibrations of any instrument are excited, by resonance, *only when vibrations of the same period are already present in the surrounding air.* Accordingly, the only sound *directly* originated in each variation of our experiment, viz. that of the note [♪], must *have contained all the tones suc-*

cessively heard. The reader should apply the method of proof here adopted to notes in various regions of the key-board. He will find considerable differences, even between consecutive notes, in the number and relative intensities of the separate tones into which he is thus able to resolve them. The higher the pitch of the fundamental tone, the fewer will the recognizable associated tones become, until, in the region above [musical notation], the notes are themselves approximately single tones. The causes of these differences will be explained, in detail, in a subsequent chapter; it is sufficient here to indicate their existence. The result arrived at, thus far, is that the sounds of the piano-forte are, in general, composite, the number of constituent tones into which they are resolvable being largest in the lower half of the instrument, and diminishing in its upper half, until, at last, no analysis is called for.

45. The above resolution has been effected by means of the principle of resonance. It can, however, be performed by the ear directly, though only to a small extent, and with less ease. In endeavouring to hear a particular constituent tone among the assemblage forming a compound sound, the best plan is, first to let the upper tone be heard by itself a few times so as to prepare the ear for the precise degree

of pitch it is to expect, and then to develope the compound sound. If, meanwhile, the observer has succeeded in keeping his attention unswervingly fixed on the tone for which he is listening, he will hear it come out clearly from the mass of tones included in the composite sound. If the pianoforte note, [♪], be thus examined, the octave, [♪], and Twelfth, [♪], can generally be recognised with considerable ease; the second octave, [♪], with a little trouble; the next three tones of the series on p. 84, with increasing difficulty, and those which succeed them not at all. The reader approaching this phenomenon for the first time must not be disappointed if, in trying this experiment, he fail to hear the tones he is told to expect. He should vary its conditions by changing the note struck, in such a way that his attention will not be liable to be diverted by the presence of distinct tones more acute than that of which he is in search. Thus a note near [♪] may be advantageously chosen to observe the first octave, [♪]; one near [♪] to observe the Twelfth, [♪]; one near [♪] to observe the second octave, 𝄞 . He may however altogether fail in performing the analysis with the unassisted ear. This by no means indicates any aural defect, as he may at first be inclined to imagine. It rather shows that the life-long habit of regarding the notes of individual sound-producing instruments as single tones cannot be unlearned all at once. The case is analogous to that of single vision with two eyes, where *two* distinct and different images are so blended together as to appear, to all ordinary observation, as *one*. The acoustical observer who is thus situated, must rely on the analysis by resonance, and on the evidence of those who are able to perform the direct analysis. As he pursues the subject further experimentally, his analytical faculty will no doubt in time adequately develope itself.

46. The composite character of musical sounds, which we have recognized in the case of the pianoforte, and shall have ample opportunity of verifying more generally in the sequel, requires the introduction, here, of certain verbal definitions and limitations. The phraseology hitherto employed, both in the science of acoustics and in the theory of music, goes on the supposition that the sounds of individual instruments are single tones, and therefore, of course, contains no term specially denoting compound sounds

and their constituents. 'Sound,' 'note,' and 'tone' are used as nearly synonymous. It will be convenient to restrict the meaning of the latter so that it shall denote a sound which does not admit of resolution into simple elements. A single sound of determinate pitch we shall, accordingly, in what follows, call a *tone*, or *simple tone*. For a compound sound the word *clang* will be a serviceable term. The series of elementary sounds into which a clang can be resolved we shall call its *partial-tones*, sometimes distinguishing, among these, the lowest, or *fundamental tone*, from the others, or *overtones* of the clang. This nomenclature is a direct adaptation of the German terms employed by Helmholtz. Its introduction is due to Professor Tyndall.

47. This long discussion has paved the way for the complete explanation of musical *quality* which is contained in the following proposition. *The quality of a clang depends on the number, orders, and relative intensities, of the partial-tones into which it can be resolved.* We have here three different causes to which variations in the quality of composite sounds are assigned.

1. A clang may contain only two or three, or it may contain half-a-dozen, or even as many as fifteen or twenty, well-developed partial-tones.

2. The *number* of partial-tones present remain-

ing the same, the quality will vary according to the positions they occupy in the fixed series on p. 84, *i.e.* on their *orders*. Thus, a clang containing *three* tones may consist of (1), (2), (3), or of (1), (3), (5), or of (1), (7), (10), and so on, the *quality* varying in each instance.

3. The *number* and *orders* of the partial-tones present remaining the same, the quality will vary according to the relative degrees of loudness with which those tones speak. Thus, in the simplest case of a clang consisting of (1) and (2), (2) may be twice as loud, or as loud, or half as loud, as (1), and so on.

It is clear that these three classes of variations are entirely independent of each other, that is to say, any two clangs may differ in the number, orders, *and* relative intensities, of their constituent partial-tones. The variety of quality thus provided for is almost indefinitely great. In order to form some idea of its extent, let us see how many clangs of different quality, but of the same pitch, can be formed with the first *six* partial-tones, by variations of *number and order only*. We will indicate each group of tones by the corresponding figures inclosed in a bracket; thus *e.g.* (1, 3, 5) represents a clang consisting of the first, third and fifth tones.

All the possible groups, each necessarily containing the same fundamental tone, are given in the following enumeration.

Two at a time:
    (1, 2), (1, 3), (1, 4), (1, 5), (1, 6).
Total 5.

Three at a time:
    (1, 2, 3), (1, 2, 4), (1, 2, 5), (1, 2, 6), (1, 3, 4),
    (1, 3, 5), (1, 3, 6), (1, 4, 5), (1, 4, 6), (1, 5, 6).
Total 10.

Four at a time:
    (1, 2, 3, 4), (1, 2, 3, 5), (1, 2, 3, 6),
    (1, 2, 4, 5), (1, 2, 4, 6), (1, 2, 5, 6),
    (1, 3, 4, 5), (1, 3, 4, 6), (1, 3, 5, 6), (1, 4, 5, 6).
Total 10.

Five at a time:
    (1, 2, 3, 4, 5), (1, 2, 3, 4, 6), (1, 2, 3, 5, 6),
    (1, 2, 4, 5, 6), (1, 3, 4, 5, 6).
Total 5.

Six at a time: (1, 2, 3, 4, 5, 6).
Total 1.

The whole number of groups is 31, or, if we allow the fundamental tone (1) to count by itself as a sound of separate quality, 32. Let us next examine how many clangs of different quality can be obtained from a single combination of three fixed partial-tones by variations of *intensity only*, supposing that each tone is capable of but *two* degrees of loudness. Representing one of these by f, and the other by p, we indicate, *e.g.*, by (f, p, p) a clang in which the fundamental tone is sounded *forte*, and the two overtones *piano*. The different cases which present themselves are the following:

$$(f,f,f), (f,p,f), (p,f,f), (p,p,f), (f,f,p),$$
$$(f,p,p), (p,f,p), (p,p,p)$$

or *seven* in all, since (p, p, p) has the same quality as (f,f,f). The number of cases increases very rapidly as we take more partial-tones together. Thus a clang of four tones will produce 15 sounds of different quality; one of five tones 31; one of six tones 63, by variations of intensity only. Altogether we could form, with six partial-tones, each susceptible of only two different degrees of intensity, upwards of *four hundred* clangs of distinct quality, all having the same fundamental tone. The supposition above made utterly understates, however, the varieties of quality dependent only on changes of relative intensity. A very slight increase, or diminution, of loudness, on the part of a single constituent tone, is enough to produce a sensible change of quality in the clang. We should be still far below the mark if we allowed each partial tone *four* different degrees of intensity, though even this supposition would bring us more than *eight thousand* separate cases. Since many more variations of intensity are practically efficacious, and also since the number of disposable partial-tones need by no means be limited, as has here been done, to the first *six*, the above calculation will probably suffice to convince the reader that the varieties of quality which the theory we are engaged upon is capable of accounting for, are almost indefinitely numerous. This is, in fact, no more than we have a right to expect from the theory, when we reflect on the fine shades of quality which the ear is able to distinguish. No two instruments of the same class are exactly alike in this respect. For instance, grand pianofortes by Broadwood and by Erard exhibit unmistakeable differences, which we describe as 'Broadwood tone' and 'Erard tone.' Less marked, but still perfectly recognizable, differences exist between individual instruments of the same class and maker, and even between consecutive notes of the same instrument. To these we have to add the variations in quality due to the manner in which the performer handles his instrument. Even on the pianoforte the kinds of tone elicited by a dull slamming touch, and by a lively elastic one, are clearly distinguishable. With other instruments the distinctions are much more marked. On the violin we perceive endless gradations of quality, from the rasping scrape of the beginner up to the smooth and superb tone of a Joachim (or, as I ought rather to say, *the* Joachim). A precisely similar remark applies to wind instruments; the differences, for example, between first-rate and inferior playing on the hautbois, bassoon, horn, or trumpet, being perfectly obvious to every musical ear.

In the next chapter we will discuss the quality and essential mechanism of the principal musical instruments, among which the pianoforte will receive an amount of attention proportionate to its popularity and general use. We begin with the elementary tones of which all composite sounds are made up.

CHAPTER V.

ON THE ESSENTIAL MECHANISM OF THE PRINCIPAL MUSICAL INSTRUMENTS, CONSIDERED IN REFERENCE TO QUALITY.

1. *Sounds of tuning-forks.*

48. When a vibrating tuning-fork is held to the ear, we perceive, beside the proper note of the fork, a shrill, ringing, and usually rather discordant, sound. If however the fork is mounted on its resonance-box, as in Fig. 24, p. 79, the fundamental tone is so much strengthened that the other is by comparison faint, and the sound heard may be regarded as practically a simple tone. It is characterised by extreme mildness, without a trace of anything which could be called harsh or piercing. As compared with a pianoforte note of the same pitch, the fork-tone is wanting in richness and vivacity, and produces an impression of greater depth, so that one is at first inclined to think the pianoforte note corresponding to it must be an octave lower than is actually the case. It follows

immediately from the general theory of the nature of quality, that simple tones can differ only in pitch and intensity. Accordingly, we find that tuning-forks of the same pitch, mounted on resonance-boxes and set vibrating by a resined fiddle-bow, exhibit, however various their forms and sizes, differences of *loudness only*. When made to sound with equal intensity by suitable bowing, their tones are absolutely undistinguishable from each other.

2. *Sounds of vibrating strings.*

49. Sounding strings vibrate so rapidly that their movements cannot be followed directly by the eye. It will be well, therefore, that we should examine how the slower and more easily controllable vibrations of non-sounding strings are performed, before treating the proper subject of this section. Take a flexible caoutchouc tube, ten or fifteen feet long, and fasten its ends to two fixed objects, so that the tube is loosely stretched between them. The tube can be set in regular vibration by impressing a swaying movement upon it with the fingers near one extremity, in suitable time. According to the rapidity of the motion thus communicated, the tube will take up different forms of vibration. The simplest of these is shown in Fig. 26. *A* and *B* being its fixed extremities, the tube vibrates *as a*

whole, between the two extreme positions *AaB* and *AbB*.

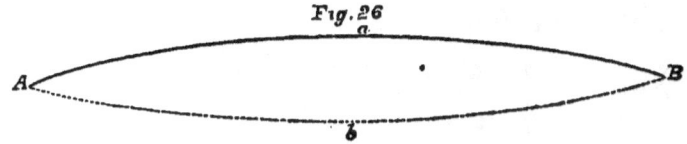

The tube may also vibrate in the form shown in Fig. 27, where *AabB* and *AcdB* are its extreme positions.

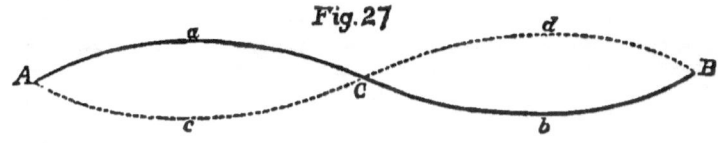

In this instance the middle point of the tube, *C*, remains at rest, the loops on either side of it moving independently, as though the tube were fastened at *C*, as well as at *A* and *B*. For this reason the point *C* is called a *node*, from the Latin *nodus*, a knot.

Fig. 28 shows a form of vibration with two nodes,

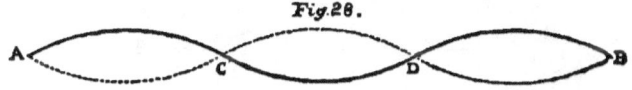

at *C* and *D*, dividing the distance *AB* into three equal parts. The portions of the tube *AC*, *CD*, *DB* vibrate independently of each other, forming what are called *ventral segments*. We may also obtain forms with three, four, five, &c., nodes, dividing the tube into four, five, six, &c., equal ventral segments, respectively. The stiffness of very short portions of the tube alone imposes a limit on the subdividing process. Let us examine the mechanical causes to which these effects are due.

50. If we unfasten one end of the tube, and, holding it in the hand as in Fig. 29, raise a hump upon it, by moving the hand suddenly through a small

Fig. 29.

distance, the hump will run along the tube until it reaches its fixed extremity B; it will then be reflected and run back to A, where it will undergo a second reflection, and so on. *At each reflection the hump will have its convexity reversed.* Thus, if while travelling from A towards B its form was that of a, Fig. 30, on its return it will have the form b. After

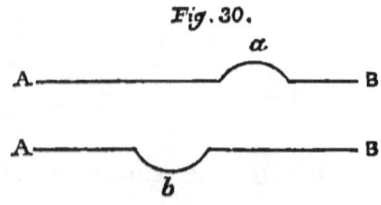

Fig. 30.

reflection at A, it will resume its first form a, and so on. Now, instead of a single jerk, let the hand holding the free end execute a series of equal continuous vibrations. Each complete vibration will cause a wave ab Fig. 31, consisting of crest b, and trough a,

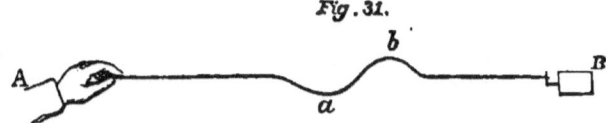

Fig. 31.

to pass along the tube from A to B, where reflection will turn crest into trough and trough into crest; so that the wave will return from B to A stern foremost. Next let the tube be again fastened at both ends, as before, and the vibrations of the hand impressed at some intermediate point, as C, Fig. 32.

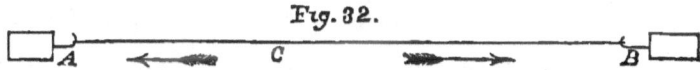

Fig. 32.

Two sets of waves will now start from C in the directions of the arrows. They will be reflected at A and B, and then their effects intermingled. We will suppose that the tube has been set in steady motion, and, the hand being removed, continues its vibrations without any external force acting on it. Two sets of equal waves are now moving with equal velocities from A towards B and from B towards A, and we have to determine their joint effect in fixing the form of vibration in which the tube swings.

Suppose that a crest a, Fig. 33, moving from A towards B, meets an equal trough b, moving from B towards A, at the point c. The point c is now solicited by a and b in opposite directions and with equal energy, and therefore remains at rest. The

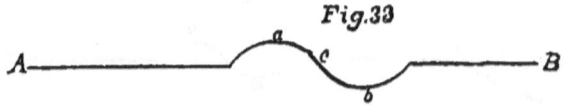

Fig. 33

two opposite pulses then proceed to cross each other, but, as a moves to the right and b to the left with equal speed, there is nothing to give either of them an influence upon the point c, where they first met, superior to that exercised in the contrary direction by the other. Thus c *remains at rest* under their joint influence, and *a node is therefore formed at that point*. If a trough had been moving from A towards B, and an equal crest from B towards A, the effect would clearly have been the same.

A node must therefore be formed at every point where two equal and opposite pulses, a crest and a trough, meet each other.

51. The annexed figure represents two series of equal waves advancing in opposite directions with equal velocities. The moment chosen is that at which crest coincides with crest and trough with trough. The joint effect thus produced does not appear in the figure, our object at present being merely to determine the number and positions of the resulting nodes. For the sake of clearness, one set of waves

is represented slightly below the other, though, in fact, the two are strictly coincident.

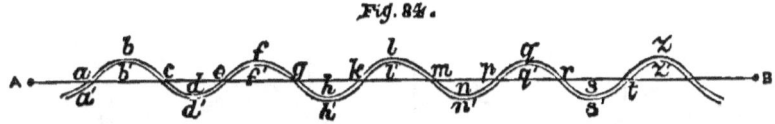

Fig. 84.

Let the waves *abdf...z* be moving from left to right, the waves *z't's'n'...a'* from right to left. The crest *klm* meets the trough *pn'm* at *m*. After these have crossed each other, the trough *ghk* and the crest *rq'p* will also meet at *m*, since *km* and *pm* are equal distances. Similarly the crest *efg* and the trough *ts'r* will meet at *m*. Accordingly the point *m* is a node, and, by exactly the same reasoning, so are *a*, *c*, *e*, *g*, *k*, *p*, *r*, *t*, &c. The distances between pairs of consecutive nodes are all equal, each being a single pulse-length, *i.e.* half a wave-length, of either series.

Two pulse-lengths, as *gk* and *km*, give *three* nodes *g*, *k*, and *m*; three pulse-lengths four nodes, and so on. There is thus always one node in excess of the number of pulses. On the other hand, the fixed ends of the tube, which are the origins of the systems of reflected waves, occupy two of these nodes. Deducting them we arrive at this result.

The number of nodes is one less than the number of the pulse-lengths (or half wave-lengths), which together make up the length of the vibrating tube.

102 NATURE OF SEGMENTAL VIBRATION. [V. § 52.

52. We will now ascertain how the portions of the tube between consecutive nodes move under the

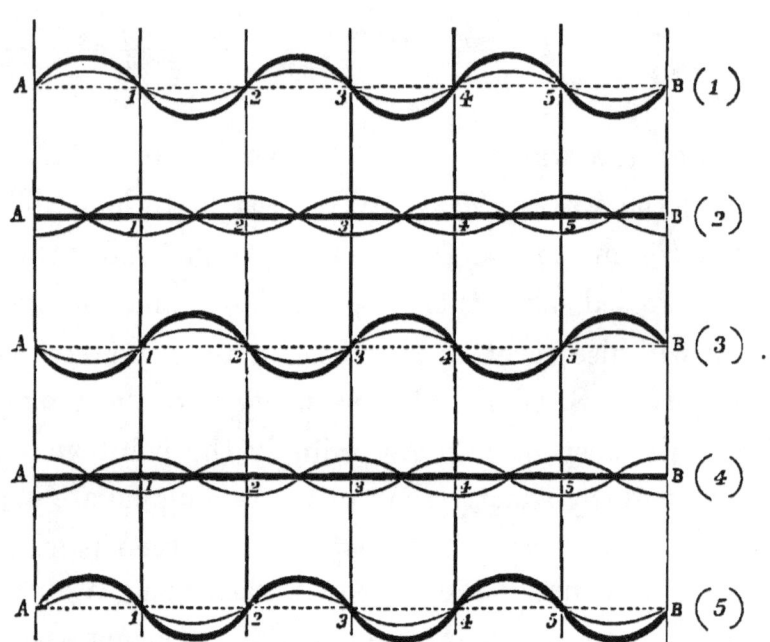

Fig. 35.

action of the two systems of waves passing along it. Let AB, Fig. 35, be the fixed ends, as before, and let us take five nodes at the points 1, 2, 3, 4, 5. In (1), the systems of waves coincide, accordingly each point of the tube is displaced through twice as great a distance as if it had been acted on by only one system. The tube thus takes the form indicated by the strong line in the figure. In (2), one set of waves has moved half a pulse-length to the right, and the other the same distance to the left. The two systems are now in complete opposition at every point, and the tube is, therefore, momentarily in its undisturbed position. In (3), each system has moved through a pulse-length, and the combined effect is again produced on the tube, but in the opposite direction to that of (1). In (4), where the systems have moved through a pulse-length and a half, the tube passes again through its undisturbed position, and, in (5), regains the position it occupied in (1), the systems of waves, meanwhile, having each traversed two pulse-lengths, or one wave-length. Thus the tube executes one complete vibration in the time occupied by a pulse in passing along a length of the tube equal to *twice one of its own ventral segments*. In other words, *the tube's rate of vibration varies as the number of segments into which it is divided*. It moves most slowly in the form shown in Fig. 26 with but a single segment; twice as fast in that of Fig. 27, when divided into two segments; three times as fast with three segments, and so on. It is easy to confirm this by direct experiment, the swaying movement of the hand on the tube needing to be twice as rapid for a form of vibration with two segments as for a form with one, and so on.

53. Instead of comparing the different rates at which the same tube vibrates, when divided into

different numbers of ventral segments, we may compare the rates of vibration of tubes of different lengths, divided into the same number of segments.

Let us take as an example the two tubes AB, CD, Fig. 36, each divided by three nodes into four

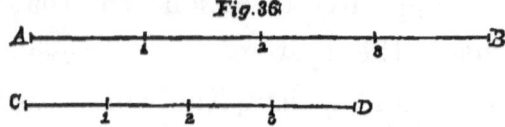

ventral segments. By what has been already shown, the time of vibration of either tube will be that which a pulse occupies in traversing two of its ventral segments. Therefore the time of vibration of AB will be to that of CD as $A2$ is to $C2$, i.e. as one half of AB is to one half of CD, or as AB is to CD. This reasoning is equally applicable to any other case. Accordingly we have the general result that, when tubes of different lengths are divided into the same number of ventral segments, their times of vibration are proportional to the lengths of the tubes, or, which comes to the same thing, their *rates of vibration inversely proportional to their lengths.* The reader should observe that it has been throughout this discussion assumed that the *material, thickness,* and *tension* of the tube, or tubes, in question, were subject to no variation whatever. Any changes in these would correspondingly affect the rates of vibration produced.

54. MOTION OF SOUNDING STRING.

54. We are now prepared to examine the motion of a sounding string. Its ends are fastened to fixed points of attachment and the string is excited at some intermediate point, by plucking it with the finger, as in the harp and guitar, by striking it with a soft hammer, as in the pianoforte, or by stroking it with a resined bow, as in the violin and other instruments of the same class. The impulses thus set up are reflected at the extremities of the string (in the violin at the bridge and at the finger of the performer) and behave towards each other exactly as in the case of the vibrating tube considered above. The results thus obtained are therefore directly applicable to the case before us. The string may vibrate in a single segment as in Fig. 26. This is the form of slowest vibration with a string of given length, material and tension. Accordingly, when thus vibrating, the string produces the deepest note of which, all other conditions remaining the same, it is capable. The string may also vibrate in the forms shown in Figs. 27, 28, 35, or in forms with larger numbers of segments. The rapidity of vibration in any one of these forms is, as we have seen [§ 52], proportional to the number of segments formed, so that, with two segments, it vibrates *twice*, with three, *thrice*, with four, *four times*, as fast as in the form with one segment. It follows

hence [§ 43] that the notes obtained by causing a string to vibrate successively in forms of vibration with 1, 2, 3, 4, 5 &c., segments are all partial-tones of one compound sound, the lowest being of course its fundamental-tone.

The modes of eliciting the sounds of stringed instruments described on p. 105 are not capable of setting up any *one* of the above forms of vibration *by itself*, but cause several of them to be executed together. The result is that each form of vibration called into existence sings, as it were, its own note, without heeding what is being done by its fellows. Accordingly, a certain number of tones belonging to one family of partial-tones are simultaneously heard.

What precise members of the general series of partial-tones [p. 84] are present, and with what relative intensities, in the sound of a string set vibrating by a blow, depends on the position of the point at which the blow is delivered, on the nature of the striking-object, and on the material of the string. It is clear that a node can never be formed at the point of percussion. Therefore no partial-tone requiring for its production a node in that place can exist in the resulting sound. If, for instance, we excite the string exactly at its middle point, the forms of vibration with an *even number* of ventral segments, all of which have a node at the centre of the string, are excluded, and only the *odd* partial-tones, i.e. the 1st, 3rd, 5th, and so on, are heard. In this manner we can always prevent the formation of any assigned partial-tone, by choosing a suitable point of percussion. On the other hand, a vibration-form is in the most favourable position for development when the *middle point* of one of its ventral segments coincides with the point of percussion. The more nearly it occupies this position the louder will be the corresponding partial-tone, while the more it recedes from this position towards that in which one of its nodes falls on the point of percussion, the weaker will the partial-tone become.

The form and material of the hammer, or other object with which the string is struck, have also a great influence in modifying the quality of the sound produced. Sharpness of edge and hardness of substance tend to develope high and powerful overtones, a rounded form and soft elastic substance to strengthen the fundamental-tone. The material of the string itself produces its effect chiefly by limiting the number of partial-tones. The stiffness of the string resists division into very short segments, and this implies, for every string, a fixed limit beyond which further submission becomes impossible; and where, therefore, the series of overtones is cut short. Hence very thin mobile strings are favourable, thick weighty strings unfavourable, to the production of a large number of partial-tones.

55. Having examined what determines the *quality* of the sound of a vibrating string, we have next to enquire on what its *pitch* depends. This term is indeed, strictly speaking, inappropriate to a composite sound containing a series of different tones, each having its own vibration-number and definite position in the musical scale. If, however, we use the phrase 'pitch of a sound' as equivalent to 'pitch of the fundamental tone of the sound,' we shall avoid any confusion arising from this circumstance. The pitch of a string-sound depends of course on the rate at which the string is vibrating. We have seen that, when the material thickness and tension of a string remain the same, its rate of vibration varies inversely as the length of the string. Accordingly, *the vibration-number of a string-sound varies inversely as the length of the string.* It follows hence that the numerical relations between the vibration-numbers of sounds forming given intervals with each other, hold equally for the lengths of the strings by which such sounds are produced. To verify this by experiment we have only to stretch a wire between two fixed points A and B, and divide it into two segments by applying the finger to it at some inter-

mediate point *C*. If *AC* bears to *CB* any one of the simple numerical ratios exhibited in the table on

p. 66, we obtain the corresponding interval there given by alternately exciting the vibrations of the two segments at any pair of points in *AC* and *CB* respectively. Thus, if *CB* is twice as long as *AC*, the sound produced by the former will be one octave lower than that produced by the latter. If *AC* is to *CB* in the proportion of 2 to 3, *AC*'s sound will be a Fifth above *CB*'s; and similarly in other cases. It was by experiments of this kind that the ancient Greek philosopher, Pythagoras, discovered the existence of a connection between certain musical intervals and the ratios of certain small integers. He ascertained that an octave was produced by a wire divided into two parts in the proportion of 2 to 1; that a Fifth was obtained by division in the proportion of 3 to 2, and so forth. The relations existing between these lengths and the vibration-numbers of the notes produced by them were entirely unknown to Pythagoras and his contemporaries; indeed it was not until the seventeenth century that they were discovered by Galileo.

In instruments of the violin class, the pitch of the notes sounded varies with the position of the finger on the vibrating string. The length of string intercepted between the fixed bridge and the finger admits of being altered at pleasure, and thus every shade of pitch can be produced from such instruments. The resined bow maintains the vibration of the string by alternately dragging it out of its position of rest, letting it fly back again, catching it once more, and so on. The hollow cavity of the instrument reinforces the string-sound by resonance. The quality of instruments of the violin class is vivacious and piercing. The first eight partial tones are well represented in their clang.

The Pianoforte.

56. In this instrument each wire is stretched between two pegs, which are fixed into a flat plate of wood called the sound-board. The string is fastened to one peg, and coiled round the other, which admits of being turned about its own axis by means of a key of suitable construction. In this manner the string can be accurately tuned, since by tightening or loosening the wire, we raise or lower its pitch at pleasure. In small instruments *two*, in larger ones *three*, wires in unison with each other usually correspond to each note of the key-board. While

the instrument is not in action a series of small pieces of wood covered with list, called 'dampers,' rest upon the wires. These are connected with the key-board in such a manner that, when a note is pressed down, the corresponding damper rises from its place, and the wires it previously covered remain free, until the note is allowed to spring up again, when the damper immediately sinks back into its original position. Each note is connected with an elastic hammer, which deals a blow to its own set of wires, and then springs back from them. The wires thus set in motion continue to vibrate until either the sound gradually dies away, or is abruptly extinguished by the descent of the damper. The action of the two pedals is as follows: the soft pedal shifts the key-board and associated hammers in such a way that each hammer only acts on *one* of the wires corresponding to it, instead of on its complete set of two or three wires. The sound produced by striking a note is therefore proportionally weakened. The loud pedal lifts all the dampers off the wires at once. It thus not only allows notes to continue sounding after the finger of the player has quitted them, but places other wires than those actually struck in a position to sound by resonance. The number of wires thus brought into play by striking a single note of the instrument will be easily seen to be considerable. Suppose, first, that a *simple-tone*, e.g. that of a tuning-fork, is sounding near the wires of a pianoforte with the loud pedal *down*, its pitch being that of middle C, 𝄞 ; the wires of the corresponding note will of course resonate with it, vibrating in the simplest form with only one ventral segment. The wires of the note 𝄢 one octave below it, are also capable of producing middle C when they vibrate in the form with two segments. So are those of 𝄢 , a Twelfth below it, when vibrating with three segments, those of 𝄢 , two octaves below it, vibrating with four segments, and so on. Proceeding in this way we determine a series of notes on the key-board of the pianoforte, the wires of which are able to produce a simple tone of the pitch of middle C. They obviously follow the same law as the harmonic overtones of a compound sound with middle C for its fundamental-tone, except that the successive intervals are reckoned *downwards* instead of upwards. The wires of all these notes will reinforce the tone of the tuning-fork by resonance. If now we remove the fork, and strike middle C on the pianoforte itself, we obtain, of course, a compound sound consisting of a number of simple tones. To each of these latter there corresponds a descending series of notes on the key-board, commencing with that whose fundamental is in unison with the simple-tone in question. A full chord struck in the middle region of the instrument will, in this way, command the more or less active services of two or three times as many wires as have been set vibrating by direct percussion. The increase of *loudness* thus secured is not very considerable, the effect being rather a heightened richness, like that of a mass of voices singing pianissimo. The actual intensity of the sound so heard may be less than could be produced by a quartett of solo singers, but it possesses a multitudinous character which the other lacks. The sustaining power of the loud pedal renders care in its employment essential. It should, as a general rule, be held down only so long as notes belonging to one and the same chord are struck. Whenever a change of harmony occurs, the pedal should be allowed to rise, in order that the descent of the dampers may at once extinguish the preceding chord. If this precaution is neglected, perfectly irreconcilable chords become promiscuously jumbled together, and a series of jarring discords ensue, which are nearly as distressing to the ear as the striking of actual wrong notes. The quality of pianoforte notes varies greatly in different parts of the scale. In the lower and middle region it is full and rich, the first six partial-tones being audibly present, though 4, 5, 6 are much weaker than 1, 2, 3. Towards the upper part of the instrument the higher partial-tones disappear, until in the uppermost octave the notes are actually simple-tones, which accounts for their tame and uninteresting character. The pianoforte shares with all instruments of fixed sounds certain serious defects, which will be discussed in detail in a subsequent chapter.

When a vibrating wire is passing through its undisturbed position, its tension is necessarily somewhat less than at any other moment, since, in order to assume the curved segmental form, it must be a little elongated, which involves a corresponding increase of tension. Hence the two pegs by which the ends of a wire are attached to the sound-board are submitted to an additional strain *twice* during each complete segmental vibration. The sound-board, being purposely constructed of the most elastic wood, yields to the rhythmic impulses acting upon it, and is thrown into segmental vibrations like those of the wire.

These vibrations are communicated to the air in contact with the sound-board, and then transmitted further in the ordinary way. The amount of surface which a wire presents to the air is so small, that, but for the aid of the sound-board, its vibrations would hardly excite an audible sound. The reader will not fail to notice that the sound-board of the pianoforte plays the same part as the hollow cavity of the violin, and is, in fact, a *solid resonator*. In the harp, the framework of the instrument serves the same purpose. We have, in this combination of a vibration-exciting apparatus with a resonator, the type of construction adopted in nearly all musical instruments.

3. *Sounds of organ-pipes.*

57. It has been shown [§ 51] that, when two series of equal waves due to transverse vibrations, travel along a stretched wire, in opposite directions, stationary nodes are formed at equal distances along it, separated by vibrating segments of equal lengths. Let us now suppose that two series of equal waves due to *longitudinal* vibrations are traversing, in opposite directions, a column of air contained in a tube of uniform bore. Each set of such waves has its own associated wave-form [§ 18]. These will behave to each other precisely in the same way as the transverse waves of Fig. 35. We have only, therefore, to consider the curves drawn in that figure as constituting the associated waves for the longitudinal air-vibrations, in order to make the conclusions of § 52 at once applicable to the case before us. The

result is a series of equidistant nodes, or points of permanent rest, distributed along the column of air. The intervening portions of air vibrate longitudinally at the same rate as the corresponding ventral segments of Fig. 35. We have here, as in the case of the sounding wire, all the conditions for the production of a musical note, of pitch corresponding to the rapidity of vibration obtained. It only remains to show that, in the case of every organ-pipe, two sets of equal waves traverse in opposite directions the air-column which it contains.

Organ pipes are of two kinds, called respectively 'stopped' and 'open,'—epithets which, however, apply only to one end of the pipe; the other is in both kinds open.

To begin with the first variety.

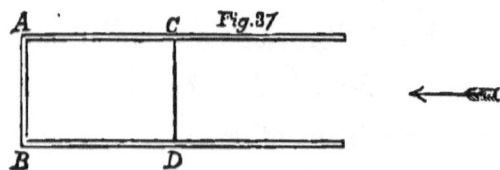

58. Let AB, Fig. 37, be the closed end of a stopped pipe, and let a series of pulses of condensation and rarefaction be passing along the air within it, in the direction shown by the arrow. First let a pulse of condensation, $CABD$, have just reached AB. By supposition, the air in AD is denser, and there-

fore at a higher pressure, than the air behind it. It will therefore expand. Forward motion being barred by AB, the expansion must take place entirely in the opposite direction. Hence the pulse of condensation is reflected at the end of the pipe, and proceeds to traverse its previous course in the reverse direction. Next, suppose $CABD$ to be a pulse of rarefaction. The air in it is at a less pressure than that of the air behind it. Accordingly, it will be condensed between the pressure from behind and the resistance of the fixed obstacle in front. The condensed pulse behind it will expand during the process and become itself rarefied. Thus a pulse of rarefaction, equally with one of condensation, is reflected at the closed end of the pipe. Neither pulse suffers any other change except of direction of motion. Since every pulse is thus regularly reflected at AB, and made to travel back unchanged along the pipe, it follows that a system of equal waves advancing in the direction of the arrow is necessarily met by an exactly equal system proceeding in the opposite direction. For stopped pipes, therefore, the point required to be proved is made out.

Let AB, Fig. 38, be one end of an open pipe, along which condensed and rarefied pulses are being alternately transmitted in the direction of the arrow. First, let $CABD$ be a pulse of condensation which has just reached AB. The air in it is at a higher pressure than the outer air beyond AB, which is in the

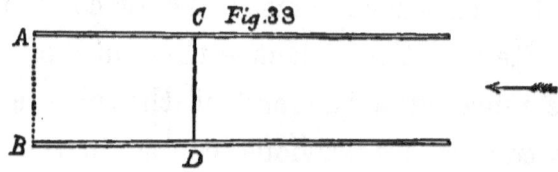

ordinary atmospheric condition, neither condensed nor rarefied. Hence some of the advanced part of the pulse $CABD$ will escape into the open air. This exit will cease as soon as the air just in front of AB has been sufficiently condensed by its means. But, in the mean time, $CABD$ has become rarefied by the escape of part of its air. Hence a rarefaction will travel back along the tube.

Now, let $CABD$ have been originally a rarefied pulse. It will be converted by the superior pressure of the air, both in front and rear, into a condensation, and in this condition start on its backward route.

By the above reasoning[1], which the student should carefully compare with that of [§ 21], it is clear that reflection takes place at an open, as well as at a closed end of a pipe; with this difference however, that in the former case condensation is turned into rarefaction and rarefaction into conden-

---

[1] I am indebted for this popular explanation of reflection at the open end of a pipe to Mr Coutts Trotter, Fellow and Tutor of Trinity College, Cambridge.

sation, so that the wave returns hind part before. We have thus established for an open pipe what was proved for a stopped one on p. 117.

59. We will now examine what forms of segmental vibration the air in a stopped pipe can adopt. Every such form must necessarily have a *node coincident with the closed end of the pipe*, since no longitudinal vibrations are possible there. The impulses constituting the series of direct waves are not, as we shall see presently, originated, like those of a pianoforte string, at some intermediate point, but enter the pipe *at its open end*. This must therefore be a point of maximum vibration. Now a glance at Fig. 35, shows that the maxima of vibration are at the middle points of the ventral segments. Hence *the centre of a segment must coincide with the open end of the pipe*.

The above considerations suffice to solve the problem before us. If the closed end of the pipe is placed at A (Fig. 35), the open end must be midway between A and 1, or between 1 and 2, 2 and 3, 3 and 4, and so on. No other forms of vibration are possible.

Fig. 39 shows the air in a stopped pipe of given length vibrating in four such ways. The vertical lines indicate the positions of the nodes. For the sake of greater clearness, the loops of the associated vibration-forms are in each case drawn in dotted lines.

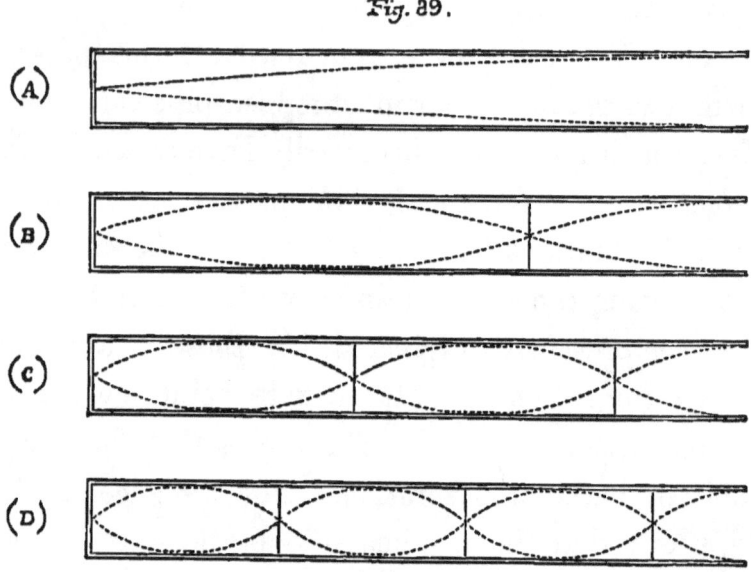

Fig. 89.

In (*A*) we have half a segment; in (*B*) a segment and a half; in (*C*) two segments and a half; in (*D*) three segments and a half. The numbers of segments into which the length of the air-column is divided, in the four cases, are, therefore, proportional to

$\tfrac{1}{2}$, $1\tfrac{1}{2}$, $2\tfrac{1}{2}$, and $3\tfrac{1}{2}$,

i.e. to $\tfrac{1}{2}$, $\tfrac{3}{2}$, $\tfrac{5}{2}$, and $\tfrac{7}{2}$,

or to the whole numbers 1, 3, 5, and 7.

Now by § 53 it appears that the rate of vibration in any form varies as the number of segments into which it is divided. The vibration-numbers of the sounds produced in the present instance are, therefore, proportional to 1, 3, 5 and 7, i. e. we get the first four *odd* partial-tones of a sound of which (A) gives us the fundamental tone [§ 43]. The reasoning here adopted evidently applies equally well to cases in which the air-column is subdivided to any assigned extent. It follows, therefore, that the notes obtainable from a stopped pipe are all odd partial-tones belonging to one and the same clang.

60. The case of the open pipe shall next be investigated. Here, as in the previous case, the end at which the direct pulses enter must be at the centre of a ventral segment. The considerations alleged on p. 118 indicate that the same thing must also hold good at the opposite orifice.

Referring once more to Fig. 35, we obtain all the possible modes of vibration which satisfy both the above conditions by placing one end of the pipe midway between A and 1, and the other successively half way between 1 and 2, 2 and 3, 3 and 4, and so on. The first four of the cases thus obtained, for a tube of constant length, are shown in the next figure, which is drawn on precisely the same plan as Fig. 39.

In each case, the two half segments at the ends of the pipe make up one whole segment. The numbers of segments into which the air-column is divided are, therefore, in (A), 1; in (B), 2; in (C), 3; in (D), 4. The same law would obviously hold for higher subdivisions. Hence, in the case of an open pipe, the rates of all the possible modes of segmental

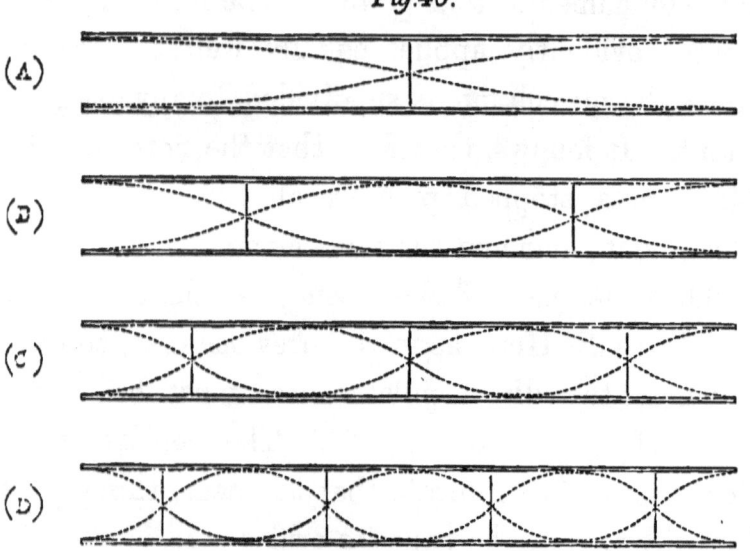

Fig. 40.

vibration are as the numbers 1, 2, 3, 4, 5, &c. The notes obtainable from such a pipe are, therefore, the *complete* series of partial-tones belonging to one and the same clang.

61. If the *slowest* forms of vibration, shown at (*A*) in Figs. 39 and 40, are compared with each other, it will be at once seen that the vibrating segment of Fig. 39 is exactly twice as long as that of Fig. 40. Hence, *the deepest tone obtainable from a stopped pipe is always precisely one octave lower than the gravest tone producible from an open pipe of the same length.* It has been shown in § 39 that this result of theory is borne out by experiment.

62. In order to complete this investigation, it is necessary to determine the pitch of the lowest note which a pipe of given length is capable of uttering. By § 52 we know that a complete segmental vibration is performed during the time occupied by a pulse in traversing *twice the length of a single segment*. In (*A*) Fig. 39, this is equal to *four times the length of the tube*. The velocity of the pulse is here the velocity of Sound in air, which, under ordinary conditions of temperature, &c., we may put at 1125 feet per second[1]. The vibration-number of a stopped pipe's lowest tone is therefore found by dividing 1125 by four times the length of the pipe expressed in feet. Conversely the length of a stopped pipe, which is to have as its deepest tone a note of given pitch, is found by dividing 1125 by four times the vibration-number of the note to be produced. The quotient gives the required length in feet. For example, middle *C* of the pianoforte makes 264 vibrations per second. The required length in this case would be expressed by $\frac{1125}{1056}$, which is rather more than 1 ft. $\frac{1}{2}$ in., i.e. roughly speaking, *one foot*. An *open* pipe, to produce the same note, would therefore have to be *two* feet in length.

It has been just shown that the vibration-number

[1] Tyndall's *Sound*, p. 24.

of the lowest tone producible, either from a stopped or an open pipe, varies inversely as the length of the pipe. The length of the pipe therefore varies inversely as the vibration-number. Hence the relations established in § 55 for strings, hold also for columns of air contained in pipes. The case of the pipe-sounds is, however, somewhat simpler than that of the string-sounds, since the pitch of the latter depends on the tension of the strings as well as on their lengths, whereas, in the former, pitch depends, under given atmospheric conditions, on length alone. Hence we may define a note of assigned pitch by merely stating the length of the stopped or open pipe, whose fundamental tone it is. The open-pipe is commonly preferred for this purpose, and accordingly organ builders call middle C '2 foot tone;' the octave below it '4 foot tone,' and so on. The lowest C on modern pianofortes is '16 foot tone;' that one octave lower, which is found only on the very largest organs, '32 foot tone.' The highest note of the pianoforte, usually A, would be about '2 inch tone.'

63. The reader should observe that, in the course of this discussion, we have incidentally obtained a more complete theory of resonance than could be given in chapter III. When a tuning-fork is held at the orifice of a tube, the strongest resonance will be produced if the note of the fork coincides with the

fundamental tone of the tube. A decided, though less powerful, resonance ought also to ensue if the fork-note coincides with one of the higher tones of the tube, which, as we know, are all overtones of its fundamental. A resonance-box is only a stopped pipe under another name. We may therefore employ it to test the truth of our result, that the only tones obtainable from a stopped pipe are the *odd* partial-tones of a clang, of which the first is the fundamental tone. I possess a series of forks giving the first seven partial-tones of a clang. When I strike 1, 3, 5 or 7, and hold them before the open end of the resonance-box corresponding to 1, a decided reinforcement of their tones is heard. If I do the same with 2, 4, or 6, hardly any resonance is produced. Thus our theoretical result is experimentally verified.

64. Organ pipes are divided into two classes according as the sounds, which they are to strengthen by resonance, are originated

(1) by blowing against a sharp edge,
(2) by blowing against an elastic tongue.

Those of the first-class are called *flue*-pipes; those of the second class *reed*-pipes. We will consider each class by itself.

65. *Flue-pipes.* Here the wind is driven through a narrow slit against a sharp edge placed exactly opposite to it, in the manner shown in Fig. 41, which

represents a vertical section of a portion of the pipe near the end at which its sound originates.

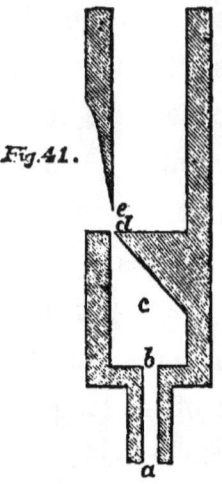

Fig. 41.

The air is forced by the bellows through the tube *ab*, into the chamber *c*, and escapes through the slit *d*, thus impinging against the edge *e*, where it produces a sharp hissing sound which may be imitated by blowing with the mouth against a knife-edge held in front of it. This sound, as we shall see in the sequel, may be regarded as consisting of a great variety of notes of different pitch. Of these the pipe is able to reinforce, by the resonance of its air-column, such notes as coincide with its own essential tones. The quality of the sound thus resulting will, of course, depend on the number, orders and relative intensities of the partial-tones present in the clang heard. The original hissing sound contributes nothing directly to the whole effect, being, with well constructed mechanism, inaudible except close to the pipe.

Stopped wooden flue-pipes of large aperture, blown by only a light pressure of wind, produce sounds which are nearly simple tones; only a trace of partial-tone No. 3 being perceptible. Such tones, like the fork tones with which they are in fact almost identical, sound sweet and mild, but also tame and spiritless. A greater pressure of wind developes 3 distinctly, in addition to 1, and, if it becomes excessive, may spoil the quality by giving the overtone too great an intensity compared to that of the fundamental, or may even extinguish the latter altogether, and so cause the whole sound to jump up an octave and a Fifth. This result may easily be obtained by blowing with the mouth into a small 6-inch stopped pipe, which can easily be obtained at any organ factory.

Stopped pipes of narrow aperture develope 5 audibly, as well as 1 and 3.

In the case of an open pipe the fundamental-tone is never produced by itself. According to the dimensions of the pipe, and the pressure of wind, it is accompanied by from two to five overtones. Open flue-pipes present, therefore, various degrees of *timbre* which are exhibited in the different 'stops' of a large organ.

66. *Reed-pipes.* The apparatus by which the sounds of pipes of this class are originated is the following. One end of a thin narrow strip of elastic metal, called a 'tongue,' is fastened to a brass plate, while the other end is free. A rectangular aperture, very slightly larger than the tongue, is cut through the plate, so as to allow the tongue to oscillate into and out of the aperture, like a door with double hinges, without touching the edges of the aperture as it passes them. The accompanying figure shows this piece of mechanism, which is called a 'reed,' in its position of rest.

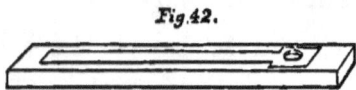

Fig. 42.

It is set in motion by a current of air being driven against the free end of the tongue, which is thus made to swing between limiting positions as shown in the annexed sections.

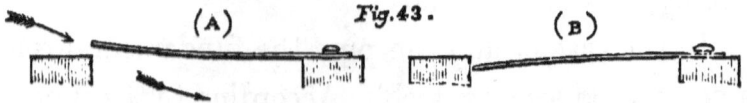

Fig. 43.

When the tongue occupies a position intermediate between that of (*A*) and its position of equilibrium, the air passes through the aperture in the direction indicated by the arrows in (*A*). At the moment that the tongue passes through its equilibrium position towards that shown in (*B*), the current of air is barred by the accuracy with which the tongue fits into the aperture beneath it. Only when the tongue again emerges can the air resume its passage. The reed thus produces a series of equal discontinuous impulses of air at equal intervals of time. The principle of the instrument is identical with that of the Syren, and it therefore gives rise to a regular musical sound. Its note is a highly composite clang, containing distinctly recognizable partial-tones up to the 16th or 20th of the series. Thus a reed does not require to be associated with a resonating column in order to produce a musical sound; in fact the instrument called the harmonium consists of reeds without such adjuncts. The *timbre* of an independent reed is, however, characterised by too great intensity on the part of the higher partial-tones. It is desirable to correct this defect by strengthening the fundamental-tone of the clang. This is done by placing the reed in the mouth of a pipe whose deepest tone coincides with the fundamental-tone of the reed-clang. This tone will then be most powerfully reinforced by resonance. The other partial-tones of the clang (the *odd* ones only in the case of a stopped pipe) will also be strengthened by resonance, but to a smaller and smaller extent as their *order* rises. The force required to throw a column of air into rapid vibration is greater than suffices to set up a slow vibration. Hence, if two partial-tones in the reed-clang were exactly equally intense, the lower of them would cause a more powerful resonance than the higher. Since the force necessary to produce segmental vibration increases very rapidly, as the subdivisions of the air-column become more numerous, the very high partial-tones of the reed-clang are practically unsupported by the resonance of the associated pipe. It will be seen hereafter how the quality of the resulting sound is improved by this circumstance.

It is clear that sounds differing widely in quality may be obtained by associating a reed with pipes of different lengths and forms. If the pipe's fundamental tone coincides with that of the reed-clang, in the case of a stopped pipe, only odd, in that of an open pipe, both odd and even, partial-tones are strengthened by resonance. If the fundamental tone of the pipe coincides with one of the *overtones* of the reed-clang, the quality of the resulting sound is correspondingly affected. The *form* of the pipe may also be modified, so as to be conical, or of any other shape, which will bring in other changes in its resonating properties. In these ways we have provision for the great variety of quality among reed-pipes, which we find represented in organ stops of that class.

4. *Sounds of orchestral wind-instruments and of the human voice.*

67. The *flute* is in principle identical with an open flue-pipe. The lips, and a hole near the end of the tube, play the parts of the narrow slit and opposing edge. The quality of the instrument is sweet, but too nearly simple to be heard during a long solo without becoming wearisome. Its most lovely effects are produced by contrast with the more brilliant *timbre* of its orchestral colleagues.

The *clarionet*, *hautbois* and *bassoon* have wooden reeds. The clarionet has a stopped cylindrical tube, producing only odd partial-tones, whence its characteristic quality. The hautbois and bassoon have conical tubes.

In the *horn* and *trumpet* the lips of the performers supply the place of a reed.

68. The apparatus of the *human voice* is essentially a reed (the vocal chords), associated with a resonance-cavity (the hollow of the mouth).

The vocal chords are elastic bands, situated at the top of the wind-pipe, and separated by a narrow slit, which opens and closes again with great exactness, as air is forced through it from the lungs. The form and width of the slit allow of being quickly and extensively modified by the changing tension of the vocal chords, and thus sounds widely differing from each other in pitch may be successively produced with surprising rapidity. In this respect, the human 'reed' far exceeds any that we can artificially construct.

The size and shape of the cavity of the mouth may be altered by opening or closing the jaws, raising or dropping the tongue, and tightening or loosening the lips. We should expect that these movements would not be without effect on the resonance of the contained air, and such proves on experiment to be the fact. If we hold a vibrating tuning-fork close to the lips, and then modify, successively, the resonating cavity, in the ways above described, we shall find that it resounds most powerfully to the fork selected when the parts of the mouth are in one definite position. If we try a fork of different pitch, the attitude of the mouth, for the strongest resonance, is no longer the same.

Hence, when the vocal chords have originated a reed-clang containing numerous well developed partial-tones, the mouth-cavity, by successively throwing itself into different postures, can favour by its resonance, first one partial-tone, then another; at one moment *this* group of partial-tones, at another *that*. In this manner endless varieties of quality are rendered possible. The art of vocalizing consists in so placing the resonating apparatus of the voice as to modify the clang due to the vocal chords in the way most attractive to the ear.

The complete analysis of the sounds of the human voice into their separate partial-tones presents peculiar difficulties to the unassisted ear, and can hardly be effected without the help of resonators such as those described in § 42. By their aid we can detect in the lower notes of a bass voice, when vigorously sung, shrill overtones reaching as far as No. 16, which is four octaves above its fundamental-tone. Under certain conditions these high overtones can be readily heard without recourse to resonators. When a body of voices are singing *fortissimo* without any instrumental accompaniment, a peculiar shrill tremulous sound is heard which is obviously far above the pitch of any note actually being sung. This sound is, to my ear, so intensely shrill and piercing as to be often quite painful. I have also observed it when listening to the lower notes of an unusually fine contralto voice. The reason why these acute sounds are tremulous will be given later.

69. We close this discussion by describing a mode of submitting Helmholtz's general theory of musical quality to a further, and very severe test.

The sounds of tuning-forks when mounted on their appropriate resonance-boxes are, as we know, very approximately simple tones. If, therefore, we allow a number of such sounds, coincident in pitch with the fundamental-tone, and with individual overtones, of one and the same clang, to be simultaneously produced, the effect on the ear ought, if Helmholtz's theory is true, to be that of a single musical sound, not that of a series of independent tones. To try the experiment in the simplest form, take two mounted forks forming the interval of an octave, and cause them to utter their respective tones together. For a short time we are able to distinguish the two notes as coming from separate instruments, but soon they blend into one sound, to which we assign the *pitch* of the *lower* fork, and a *quality* more brilliant than that of either. So strong is the illusion, that we can hardly believe the higher fork to be really still contributing its note, until we ascertain that placing a finger on its prongs at once changes the *timbre*, by reducing it to the dull, uninteresting quality of a simple tone. The character of a clang consisting of only one overtone and the fundamental, may be shown to admit of many different shades of quality, by suitably varying the relative intensities of the two fork-tones in this experiment. If we add a fork a Fifth above the higher of the first two, and therefore yielding the third partial-tone of the clang of which they form the first and second, the three tones blend as perfectly as the two did before; the only difference perceptible being an additional increase of brilliancy. The experiment admits of being carried further with the same result.

If we were able to produce by means of tuning-forks as many simple tones of the series on p. 84 as we pleased, and also to control at will their relative intensities, it would be possible to imitate, in this manner, the varying *timbre* of every musical instrument. The unmanageable character of very high forks has as yet prevented this being done for sounds containing a very large number of powerful overtones, but an apparatus on this principle has been devised by Professor Helmholtz, which imitates, very successfully, sounds not involving more than the first six or eight partial-tones. His theory of quality is thus experimentally demonstrated, both analytically and synthetically. We will examine in the next chapter some important theoretical considerations by which this theory is further elucidated and confirmed.

CHAPTER VI.

ON THE CONNECTION BETWEEN QUALITY AND MODE OF VIBRATION.

70. It was stated on p. 71 that, when a pendulum performs oscillations whose extent is small compared to the length of the pendulum itself, the *period of a vibration is the same for any extent of swing within this limit*. We will apply this fact to prove that the prongs of a tuning-fork vibrate in the same *mode* (§ 11) as does a pendulum.

When a sustained simple tone is being transmitted by the air, we may regard it as originated by a tuning-fork of appropriate pitch and size. But we know experimentally that, by suitable bowing, we may elicit from such a fork tones of various degrees of intensity, though having all the same pitch. Here, therefore, the *extent of vibration varies*, while the *period remains constant*, which is the pendulum-law. Accordingly the vibrations of a tuning-fork are identical, in *mode*, with those of a pendulum. The same thing will hold good of the aerial vibrations to which those of a fork give rise. Hence, in general, a simple tone is due to vibrations executed according to the pendulum-law.

Such vibrations when performed longitudinally, will, therefore, give rise to waves of condensation and rarefaction whose associated wave-form is that drawn in Fig. 17 (*a*) p. 38. It will be convenient to call the vibrations to which a simple tone is due *simple vibrations;* and the associated waves *simple waves.* We proceed to examine the modes of vibration corresponding to composite sounds.

Let us, first, take the case of a sustained clang consisting of but *two* simple tones, the fundamental and its first overtone. A particle of air engaged in transmitting this sound is simultaneously acted upon by two sets of vibratory movements, and we have to investigate what its motion will be under their joint influence. In fact, the problem before us is the *composition of two simple vibrations.* In order to solve it, we must employ a principle of Mechanics, called the "superposition of small motions," the nature of which can be illustrated experimentally as follows.

71. Suppose a cork to be floating on the undisturbed surface of a sheet of water into which two stones are thrown at different points. From each origin of agitation concentric circular waves will spread out, and presently the cork will be influenced by both sets of disturbances at once. Either series of waves, if it acted separately on the cork, would cause it to execute a vibratory movement in a verti-

cal straight line. The mechanical principle which we are explaining asserts that the joint effect of the two sets on the cork will be exactly equal to the sum or difference of their separate effects, according as these are produced in the same, or in opposite directions. The accompanying figures show the four different cases which may arise. In each, a and b are the points which the cork, originally at rest at O in the level-line, would occupy, at the moment indicated in the figure, were it acted on by either set of waves alone; c is its contemporaneous position under their joint action.

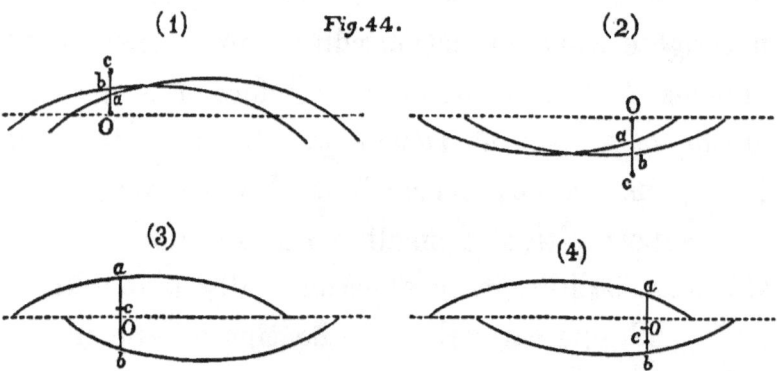

Fig. 44.

In (1), crest falls on crest; in (2), trough on trough, and the displacement, Oc, of the cork from its position of rest, O, is equal to the *sum* of the displacements due to the two crests separately, viz. Oa and Ob. In (3) and (4), where the crest of one wave meets the trough of another, Oc is equal to the *difference* between Oa and Ob; c being above or below the level-line, according as Oa is greater than Ob, as in (3), or less than Ob, as in (4). Thus, each wave produces its own full effect on the cork in its own direction, or, in other words, the motion due to one wave is 'superposed' on that due to the other.

In order, then, to determine the form of the joint wave which results from the combination of two constituent waves, we have only to apply the above principle successively to points in the level-line which both sets of disturbances simultaneously affect. We thus obtain an assemblage of points constituting the joint wave required.

In the instance now before us we proceed as follows. Let each simple tone be represented by its associated wave-system. Ascertain by the process just described to what joint form the combination of the two associated wave-systems lead. The result will be the associated system corresponding to the mode of particle-vibration to which the compound sound is due.

72. Before, however, we can lay down the two tributary systems of waves, an important point remains to be settled. We will, for a moment, suppose that the two simple tones on which we are engaged are originated and sustained by two tuning-forks,

situated as in the annexed figure, and that we are examining the transmission of their resulting clang along the dotted line with respect to which they are symmetrically situated.

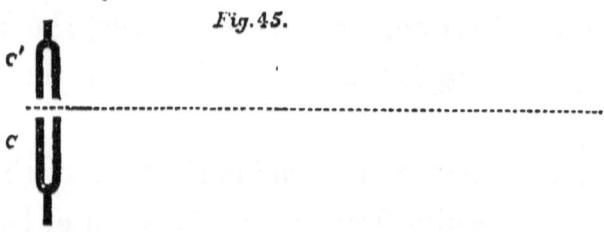

Fig. 45.

Let the forks have been set sounding by precisely simultaneous blows. They will then commence swinging out of their positions of rest *in the same direction at the same instant*. The points in the associated wave-forms where a vibrating particle is momentarily in its position of rest, are those in which it cuts the level-line. Hence, in laying down the two tributary wave-systems along the same level-line, we must make them both cut that line in *some one point*, taking care that their convexities at that point are both turned the same way, as at O, Fig. 46.

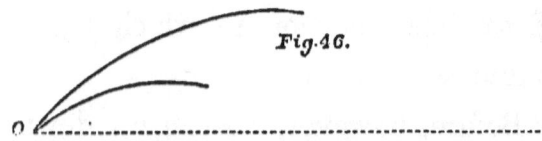

Fig. 46.

In this case the two vibrations are said to start in the *same phase*.

If the two forks are set in vibration at *different* moments, they may *not* swing out of their equilibrium positions in the same direction together. Hence we no longer necessarily have a point where both sets of waves cut the level-line. The result is of the kind shown in Fig. 47, where three different cases are represented.

Here we have vibrations starting in *different phases*.

It is clear from the figure that all phase-differences can be properly represented by merely causing the wave-systems engaged to assume different positions upon the level-line, *with reference to each other*. The second and third cases are obtainable from the first by sliding the system of shorter waves bodily along the level-line, while the other system of waves retains its position.

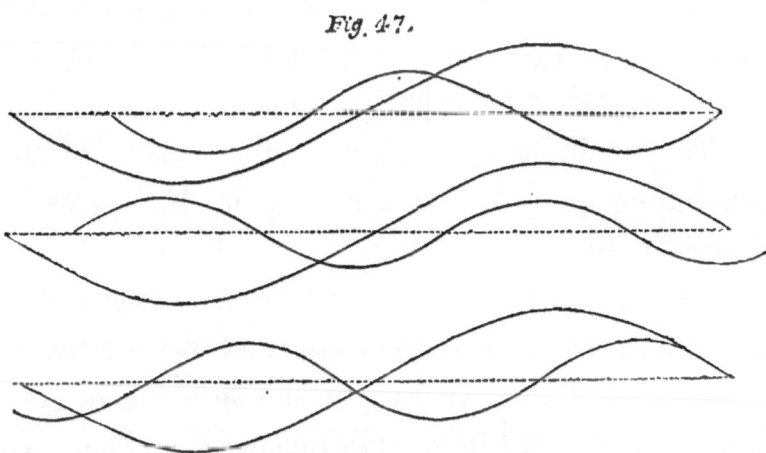

Fig. 47.

By the help of the instrument mentioned on p. 135 Professor Helmholtz has demonstrated that, when a number of partial-tones are independently produced, the clang into which they coalesce has *the same quality, whatever differences of phase may exist among the systems of simple vibrations to which the constituent partial-tones are due.* Accordingly, we may expect to find that not *one single wave-form*, but *many such forms*, correspond to a sound of given quality and pitch.

In Figs. 48, 49, 50, the associated wave-form corresponding to our clang of two partial-tones (p. 137) is constructed for three degrees of phase-difference. The simple constituent waves are shown in thin, the result of their composition in full lines. In each case two complete wave-lengths of the latter are exhibited.

Figs. 51 and 52 present two wave-forms drawn, in the same way, for a clang of constant pitch and quality containing the partial-tones 1, 2 and 3.

The dissimilarity of form, and therefore of corresponding particle-vibration, is, in both sets of figures, most marked.

73. It has been shown that, by mere alteration of phase, a very great variety of resultant wave-forms can be obtained from two sets of simple waves of given lengths and amplitudes. *Each one of these forms* will give rise to a cycle of others, if we allow the relative amplitudes of the constituent systems to be changed,

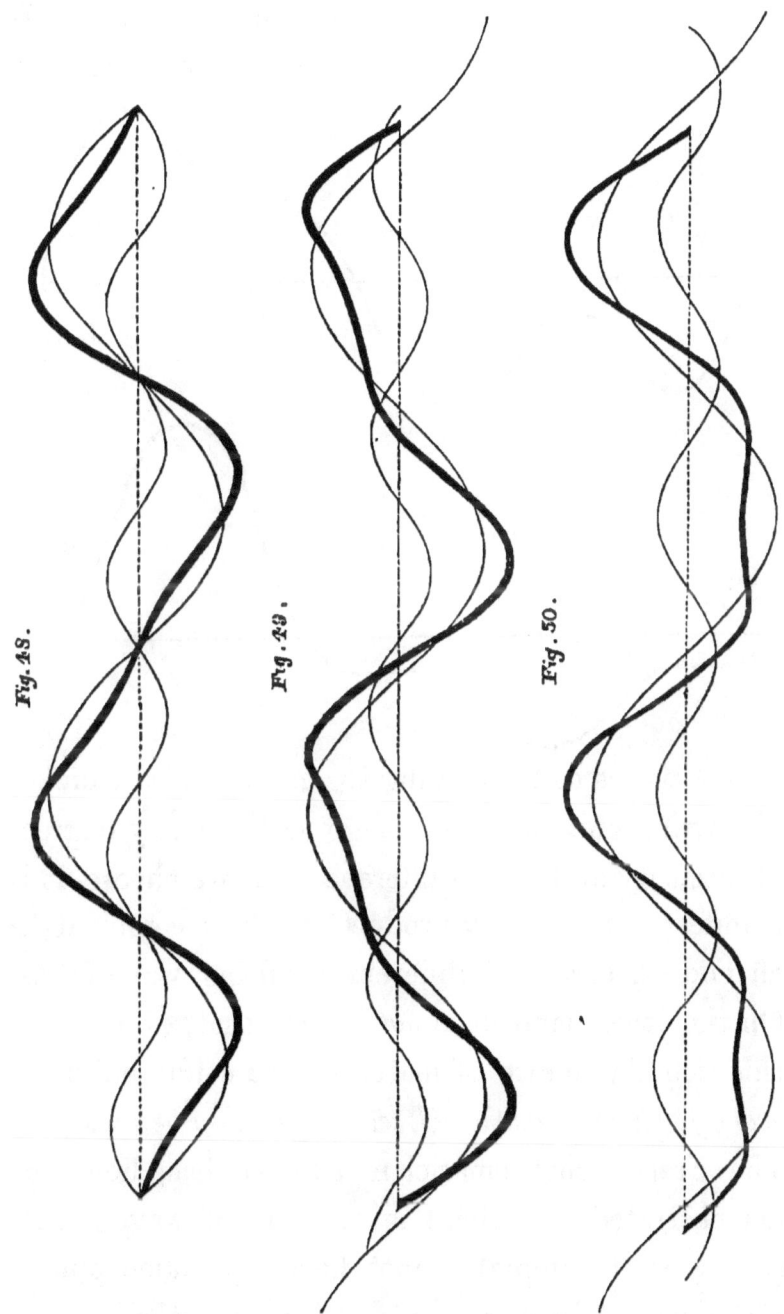

Fig. 48.

Fig. 49.

Fig. 50.

while keeping the difference of phase constant. If, therefore, we have at our disposal the systems of

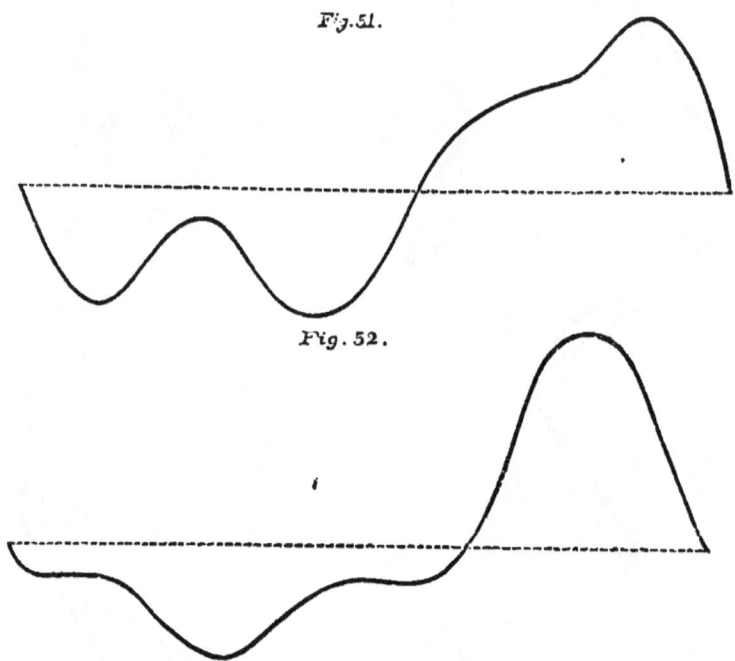

Fig. 51.

Fig. 52.

simple waves corresponding to an unlimited number of partial-tones, and can assign to them any degrees of intensity and phase-difference that we choose, it is manifest that we may produce by their combination an endless series of different resulting wave-forms. On the other hand, it is *not evident* that, even out of this rich abundance of materials, we could build up *every form of wave which could possibly be assigned*. The French mathematician *Fourier* has, however, demonstrated that there is no form of wave which (unless itself simple) cannot be compounded out of a number of simple waves, whose lengths are inversely as the numbers 1, 2, 3, 4, &c. He has further shown that each individual wave-form admits of being thus compounded in *only one way*, and has provided the means of calculating, in any given case, *how many*, and *what*, members of the partial series will appear, their relative amplitudes and their differences of phase.

When translated from the language of Mechanics into that of Acoustics, the theorem of *Fourier* asserts that every regular musical sound is resolvable into a definite number of simple tones whose relative pitch follows the law of the partial-tone series. It thus supplies a theoretical basis for the analysis and synthesis of composite sounds which have been experimentally effected in chapters IV. and V.

When we are listening to a sustained clang, the air, at any one point within the orifice of the ear, can have only one definite mode of particle-vibration at any one moment. How does the ear behave towards any such given vibration? It proceeds as follows. If the vibration is simple, it leaves it alone. If composite, it analyzes it into a series of simple vibrations whose rates are once, twice, three times &c. that of the given vibration, in accordance with Fourier's theorem. In the former event, the ear perceives only a simple tone. In the latter, it is able to recognize, by suitably directed and assisted efforts, partial-tones corresponding to the rate of each constituent into which it has analysed the composite vibration originally presented to it. The ear being deaf to differences of *phase* in partial-tones (p. 142), perceives no distinction between such modes of vibration as those exhibited on p. 143, but merely resolves them into the same single pair of partial-tones. Since, however, only *one* such resolution of a given vibration-mode is possible, the ear can never *vary* in the series of partial-tones to which it reduces an assigned clang.

The power possessed by the ear of thus singling out the constituent tones of a clang, and assigning to them their relative intensities, is unlike any corresponding capacity of the eye. Take for instance the two curves shown in Figs. 51 and 52, and try to determine, by the eye alone, what simple waves, present with what amplitudes, must be superposed in order to reproduce those forms. The eye will be found absolutely to break down in the attempt.

We have seen that the *loudness* of a composite sound depends on *extent* of vibration, and its *pitch* on *rate* of vibration. There remains only one variable element, viz. *mode* of vibration, to account for the *quality* of the sound. From this consideration it follows that *some connection* must exist between the quality of a sound and the mode of aerial vibration to which the sound is due. Up to the time of Helmholtz no advance had been made in clearing up the *nature* of this connection. It was reserved for him to show that, while no two sounds of different quality can correspond to the same mode of vibration, many different modes of vibration may yet give rise to a sound of only one degree of quality. In other words, mode of vibration determines quality, but quality does not determine mode of vibration.

CHAPTER VII.

ON THE INTERFERENCE OF SOUND, AND ON 'BEATS'.

74. In § 71 we examined the principle on which the problem of the composition of vibrations is generally solved. We now approach certain very important particular cases of that problem, which it will be worth while to solve both independently, and also as instances of the method repeatedly applied in § 72.

Suppose that a particle of air is vibrating between the extreme positions A and B, under a

Fig.53.

A B

sustained simple tone produced by a tuning-fork, or stopped flue-pipe. Now let a second instrument of the same kind be caused to emit a tone *exactly in unison with the first*. We will assume that, when the vibrations constituting the second tone fall on the particle, it is just on the point of starting from A towards B, under the influence of those of the first. Two extreme cases are now possible, depending on the movement which the particle would have executed, had it been affected by the later-impressed vibration alone. First, suppose *that* to be from A along the line AB, either through a greater or less distance than AB, back again to A, and so on. Here the separate effects of the two sets of vibrations will be *added together*, the particle will, therefore, perform vibrations of *larger extent* than it would under either component separately. Next, suppose that, under the second set of vibrations alone, the particle would move from A in the opposite direction to its former course, i.e. along BA produced, shown by a dotted line in the figure. In this case the separate effects are absolutely antagonistic; accordingly the joint result is that due to the *difference* of its components. The particle will, therefore, execute *less extensive* vibrations than it would have done under the more powerful of the two components acting alone.

The most striking result presents itself when the two systems of vibrations, besides being in complete opposition to each other, are also exactly equal in extent. In this case, the air-particle, being solicited with equal intensity in two diametrically opposite directions, remains at rest, the two systems of vibrations completely neutralizing each other's effect. In general, however, these systems, even when equal in extent of vibration, are neither in complete opposition nor in complete accordance, but in an intermediate attitude, so as only partially to counteract, or support, each other. These conclusions admit of being exhibited in a more complete manner by means of associated waves. We have only to lay down the simple wave-forms corresponding to the constituent vibrations, and superpose them as in § 72. The reader will have noticed that the differences of relative motion described on p. 149 are merely phase-differences.

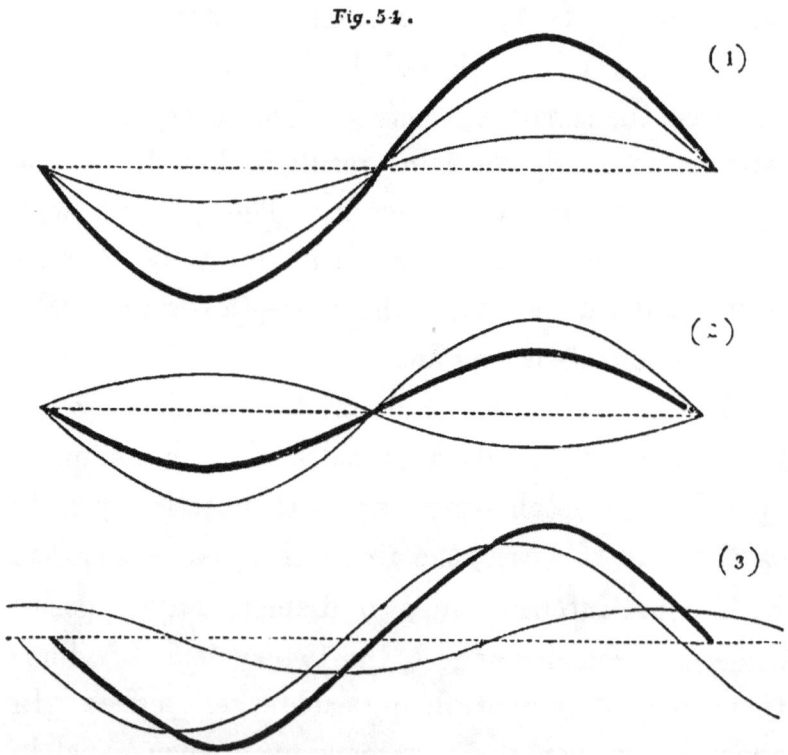

Fig. 54.

In Fig. 54, (1), (2), (3), we have two waves of

unequal amplitudes in complete accordance, complete antagonism, and an intermediate condition respectively. In Fig. 55, a case of equal and opposite waves is shown. In (1) Fig. 54, the resultant wave is the *sum*, and in (2) the *difference* of the component waves. In (3), we get a wave of intermediate amplitude. These three resulting waves are necessarily *simple*, as otherwise two simple tones in unison would give rise to a composite sound, which would be absurd. In Fig. 55 the wave-form degenerates into the level-line, i.e. no effect whatever occurs.

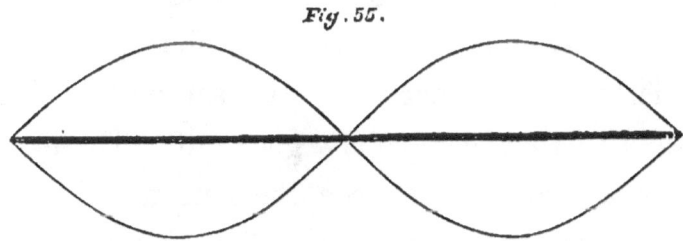

Fig. 55.

75. Thus, when one simple tone is being heard, we by no means *necessarily* obtain an increase of loudness by exciting a second simple tone of the same pitch. On the contrary, we *may* thus weaken the original sound, or even *extinguish it entirely*. When this occurs we have an instance of a phenomenon which goes by the name of *Interference*. That *two sounds should produce absolute silence* seems, at first sight, as absurd as that two loaves should be equivalent to no bread. This is, however,

only because we are accustomed to think of Sound as something with an external objective existence; not as consisting merely in a state of motion of certain air-particles, and therefore liable, on the application of an opposite system of equal forces, to be absolutely annihilated.

A single tuning-fork presents an example of this very important phenomenon. Each prong sets up vibrations corresponding to a simple tone, and the two notes so produced are of the same pitch and intensity. If the fork, after being struck, is held between the finger and thumb, and made to revolve slowly about its own axis, four positions of the fork with reference to the ear will be found where the tone completely goes out. These positions are mid-way between the four in which the faces of the prongs are held flat before the ear. As the fork revolves from one of these positions of loud tone to that at right-angles to it, the sound gradually wanes, is extinguished in passing the Interference-position, reappears very feebly immediately afterwards, and then continues to gain strength until its quarter of a revolution has been completed.

76. The case of coexistent unisons has now been adequately examined: we proceed to enquire what happens when two simple tones *differing slightly in*

pitch, are simultaneously produced. The problem is, in fact, to compound two sets of pendulum-vibrations whose periods are no longer exactly equal. Let us fix on a moment of time at which the two component vibrations simultaneously soliciting an assigned particle of air are in complete accordance, and suppose that the particle, under their joint influence, is just commencing a vibration from left to right. It will be convenient to call this an *outward*, and its opposite an *inward* swing. Since the periods of the two component vibrations are unequal, one of them will at once begin to gain on the other, and therefore, directly after the start, they will cease to be in complete accordance. It is easy to ascertain what their subsequent bearing towards each other will be, by considering two ordinary pendulums of unequal periods, both beginning an outward swing at the same instant. Let A be the slower, B the quicker pendulum. When A has just finished its outward swing, B will have already turned back and performed a portion of its next inward swing. Thus, during each successive swing of A, B will gain a certain distance upon it. When B has, in this manner, gained one whole swing, i.e. half a complete oscillation, upon A, it will begin an inward swing *at the moment when A is commencing an outward swing*. The two vibrations are here, for the moment, in *com-*

plete opposition. After another interval of equal length, B, having gained another whole swing, will be one complete oscillation ahead of A, and they will therefore start on the next outward swing together, i.e. the vibrations will be momentarily in *complete accordance.* Thus, during the time requisite to enable B to perform one entire oscillation more than A, there occur the following changes. Complete accordance of vibrations, lasting only for a single swing of the more rapid pendulum, followed by partial accordance, in its turn gradually giving way to discordance, which culminates in complete opposition at the middle of the period, and then, during its latter half, gradually yields to returning accordance, which regains completeness just as the period closes.

It follows from this, combined with what is said on p. 149, that in the case of two simple tones, we must hear a sound going through regularly recurring alternations of loudness in equal successive intervals of time, its greatest intensity exceeding, and its least intensity falling short of, that of the louder of the two tones. Each recurrence of the maximum intensity is called a *beat*, and it is clear that exactly *one* such beat will be heard in each interval of time during which the acuter of the two simple tones performs *one* more vibration than the graver tone. Accordingly, the number of beats heard in any assigned time will be equal to the number of complete vibrations which the one tone gains on the other in that time. We may express this result more briefly as follows: *the number of beats per second due to two simple tones is equal to the difference of their respective vibration-numbers.*

77. By means of the associated wave-forms we can obtain a graphic representation of beats, which will probably be more directly intelligible than any verbal description. In Fig. 56, the constituent simple waves are laid down, and their resultant constructed, for the interval of a semi-tone. The vibration-fraction for this interval is $\frac{16}{15}$; *i.e.* 16 vibrations of the higher tone are performed in the same time as 15 of the lower. The figure represents completely the state of things from a *maximum* of intensity to the adjacent *minimum*. The time during which this change occurs is one-half of that above-mentioned: accordingly the figure shows 8 and 7½ wave-lengths of the respective systems. Thus *half a beat* is here pictorially represented, the amplitude of the resultant waves steadily diminishing during this period. We have only to turn the figure upside down, to get a picture of what occurs in the next following equal period. The amplitudes here again increase, until they

regain their former proportions. *One whole beat* is thus accounted for.

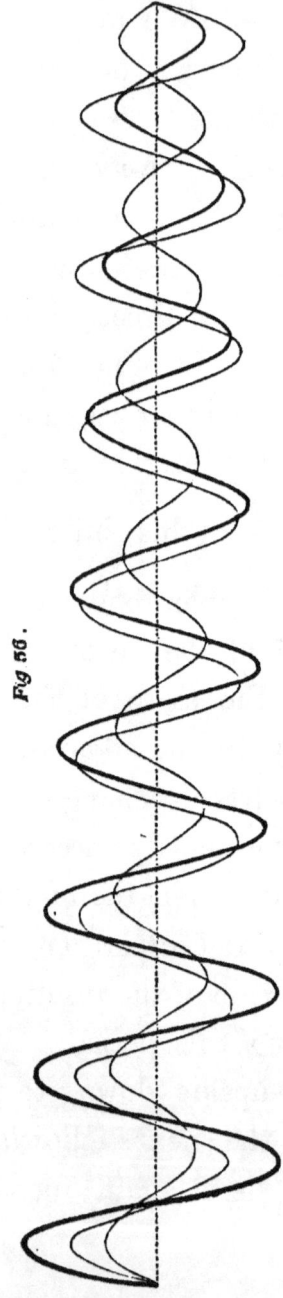

Fig 56.

In addition to the alternations of intensity which characterize beats, they also contain variations of pitch. The existence of such variations is both theoretically demonstrable and experimentally recognizable, but they are too minute to require examination here[1].

78. The most direct way of studying the beats of simple tones experimentally is to take two unison tuning-forks and attach a small pellet of wax to the extremity of a prong of one of them. The fork so operated on becomes slightly heavier than before; its vibrations are therefore proportionately retarded, and its pitch lowered. When *both* forks are struck and held to the ear beats are heard. These will be most distinct when the fork's tones are exactly equally loud, for in this case the minima of intensity will be equal to zero, and the beats will therefore be separated by intervals of absolute, though but momentary, silence. The increase, in rapidity, of the beats, as the interval between the beating-tones widens, may be shown by gradually loading one of the forks more and more heavily with wax pellets, or by a small coin pressed upon them. If it is desired

---

[1] The reader may, if he wishes to pursue this subject, refer to a paper, by the author, on '*Variations of Pitch in Beats,*' in the *Philosophical Magazine* for July, 1872, from which Fig. 56 has been copied.

to exhibit these phenomena to a large audience, the forks should first be mounted on their resonance-boxes, and, after the pellets have been attached, stroked with the resined bow, care being taken to produce tones as nearly as possible equal in intensity. Slow beats may also be obtained from any instrument capable of producing tones whose vibration-numbers differ by a sufficiently small amount. Thus, if the strings corresponding to a single note of the pianoforte are not strictly in unison, such beats are heard on striking the note. If the tuning is perfect, a wax pellet attached to one of the wires will lower its pitch sufficiently to produce the desired effect. Beats not too fast to be readily counted arise between adjacent notes in the lower octaves of the harmonium, or, still more conspicuously, in those of large organs. They are also frequently to be heard in the sounds of church bells, or in those emitted by the telegraph wires when vibrating powerfully in a strong wind. In order to observe them in the last instance, it is best to press one ear against a telegraph-post and close the other: the beats then come out with remarkable distinctness. It should be noticed that, when we are dealing with two composite sounds, several sets of beats may be heard at the same time, if pairs of partial-tones are in relative positions suited to produce them. Thus, suppose that two clangs coexist, each of which possesses the first six partial-tones of the series audibly developed. Since the second, third, &c. partial-tones of each clang make twice, three times &c. as many vibrations per second as their respective fundamentals (p. 83), it follows that the difference between the vibration-numbers of the two second-tones will be *twice*, that between those of the two third-tones *three times*, &c. as great as the difference between the vibration-numbers of the two fundamentals. Accordingly, if the fundamental tones give rise to beats, we may hear, in addition to the series so accounted for, five other sets of beats, respectively twice, three, four, five, and six times as rapid as they. In order to determine the number of beats per second, for any such set, we need only multiply the number of the fundamental beats by the *order* of the partial-tones concerned. The beats of two simple tones necessarily become more rapid if the higher tone be sharpened, or the lower flattened; i. e. if the interval they form with each other be widened. The beats may, however, also be accelerated, without altering the interval, by merely placing it in a higher part of the scale. In this way greater vibration-numbers are obtained, and the difference of these is proportionally large, though their ratio to each other remains what it was before. Thus the rapidity of the beats due to an assigned interval depends jointly on two circumstances, the width of the interval, and its position in the musical scale; in other words, on both the *relative* and *absolute* pitch of the tones forming the given interval.

CHAPTER VIII.

ON CONCORD AND DISCORD.

79. A question of fundamental importance now presents itself, viz. *What becomes of beats, when they are so rapid that they can no longer be separately perceived by the ear?* In order to answer it, the best plan is to take two unison-forks, of medium pitch, mounted on their resonance-boxes, attach a small pellet of wax to a prong of one of them, and then gradually increase the quantity of wax. At first very slow beats are heard, and as long as their number does not exceed four or five in a second, the ear can follow and count them without difficulty. As they become more rapid the difficulty of counting them augments, until at last they cannot be recognized as distinct strokes of sound. Even so, however, the ear retains the conviction that the sound it hears is a series of rapid alternations, and not a continuous tone. Its intermittent *character* is not lost, although the intermittances themselves pass

by too rapidly for individual recognition. Exactly the same thing may be observed in the *roll* of a side drum, which no one is in danger of mistaking for a continuous sound.

Rapid beats produce a decidedly harsh and grating effect on the ear; and this is quite what the analogy of our other senses would lead us to expect. The disagreeable impressions excited in the organs of sight by a flickering unsteady light, and in those of touch by tickling or scratching, are familiar to every one. The effect of rapid beats is, in fact, identical with the sensation to which we commonly attach the name of *discord*. Let us examine, in somewhat greater detail, the conditions necessary for its production between two simple-tones. If we take a pair of middle C unison forks, and gradually throw them more and more out of tune with each other in the way already described, the roughness due to their beats reaches its maximum when the interval between them is about a halftone: for a whole tone, it is decidedly less marked, and when the interval amounts to a Minor Third, scarcely a trace of it remains. Hence, in order that dissonance may arise between two simple-tones, they must form with each other a narrower interval than a minor third. If we call this interval the *beating-distance* for two such tones, we may express the above condition thus. Dissonance can arise directly between two simple tones, *only when they are within beating-distance of one another*. It follows at once from this that the amount of discord heard by no means exclusively depends on the rapidity of the beats produced, since the same interval will give rise to a very different number of beats per second according as it occupies a high or a low position in the scale. Nevertheless this circumstance exerts a considerable influence in modifying the intensity of the dissonance of given intervals, according to the absolute pitch of the tones which form them. Thus the beats of a whole tone, which, in low positions, are powerful and distinct, become less marked as we ascend in the scale, and in its highest portions practically inaudible. Accordingly the beating-distance, which, for tones of medium pitch, we have roughly fixed at a Minor Third, must be supposed to contract somewhat for very high tones, while, for very low ones, it correspondingly expands. In consequence of this, a difference of relative pitch, which, in the lower part of the scale produces beats so slow as not perceptibly to interfere with smoothness of unison, may, in its higher region cause a harsh dissonance. We have here the reason why the ear is more sensitive to slight variations of pitch in high than in low notes, and why, therefore, greater accuracy in tuning is essential to obtain a good unison effect from the former, than from the latter.

The general partial-tone series consists of simple tones which, *up to the seventh*, are mutually out of beating-distance: above the seventh they close in rapidly upon each other. In the neighbourhood of 10, the interval between adjacent partial-tones is about a whole tone; near 16, a semi-tone; higher in the series they come to still closer quarters. These high partial-tones are therefore so situated as to produce harsh dissonances with each other. Where they are strongly developed in a clang, there will therefore be a certain inevitable roughness in its *timbre*. This is the cause of the harsh quality of trumpet or trombone notes, and also of the shrill tremulous sounds sometimes observed in the human voice (p. 133). In fact we may regard all the portion of the partial-tone series above the eighth tone as contributing mere noise to the clang. Thus a noise may, conversely, be regarded as due to many simple tones within beating distance of each other.

80. It has been shown that, when two simple tones are simultaneously sustained, beats can arise directly between them only under one condition, viz. that the tones shall differ in pitch by less than a Minor Third, or thereabouts. When, however, the

two co-existing sounds are no longer simple tones, but composite clangs, each consisting of a series of well developed partial-tones, the case becomes altogether different. Let us examine the state of things which then presents itself.

The sounds of most musical instruments do not contain more than the first six partial-tones; we will, therefore, assume this to be the case with the clangs before us. No beats can then arise between partial-tones of the *same clang* for the reason assigned on p. 164. Dissonance due to beats will, however, be produced if a partial-tone belonging to one clang is within the specified distance of a partial-tone belonging to the other clang. Several pairs of tones may be thus situated, and, if so, each will contribute its share of roughness to the general effect. The intensity of the roughness due to any such pair will depend chiefly on the respective orders to which the beating partial-tones belong, and on the interval between them. The lowest partial-tones being the loudest, produce the most powerful beats, and half-tone beats are, in general, harsher than those of a whole tone. In determining the general effect of a combination of two clangs, we have to ascertain what pairs of partial-tones come within beating-distance, and to estimate the amount of roughness due to each pair. The sum of all these roughnesses, if there are several such pairs, or the roughness of a single pair if there be but one, constitutes the *dissonance of the combination*. If there be *no dissonance*, the combination is described as a *perfect concord*. When dissonance is present, it will depend on its *amount* whether the combination is called an *imperfect concord* or a *discord*. The line separating the two must, of course, be somewhat arbitrarily drawn.

81. Let us examine the principal consonant intervals, in the manner above described, beginning with the *octave*.

The minims here represent the fundamental-tones; the crotchets above them corresponding overtones. Those belonging to the higher clang are only written down as far as the third, since the fourth, fifth, and sixth have no corresponding tones of the lower clang disposable with which to form beating pairs. As long as the tuning is perfect each partial-tone of the higher clang coincides exactly with one belonging to the lower. No dissonance can consequently occur, and the combination is a perfect concord. But, suppose the higher *C* to be out of tune: each of its partial tones will be correspondingly too sharp or too flat, and three sets of beats will be heard between the partial-tones 2—1, 4—2, and 6—3. When the higher *C* is as much as a semi-tone wrong, the result is

The pair 2—1 is of the most importance, and gives in each case *sixteen beats per second*. The two others give respectively 32 and 48 beats per second. A semi-tone corresponds to about maximum roughness in the middle region of the scale, so that we have before us an exceedingly harsh discord. As the pitch of the higher note is gradually corrected, the rapidity of the beats diminishes, but the tuning must be extremely accurate to make them entirely vanish. If the note makes but *one vibration per second* too many, or too few, which corresponds to a difference in pitch of only about a *thirtieth part of a whole tone*, the defect of tuning makes itself felt by three sets of beats, of 1, 2, and 3 per second respectively. The tunist must keep slightly altering the pitch until he at length hits on that which completely extinguishes the beats. We saw in an earlier part of this inquiry (p. 63) that, when two sounds form with each other the interval of an octave, their vibration-numbers must be in the ratio of $2:1$. Long after it had been experimentally ascertained that rigorous compliance with this arithmetical condition was essential for securing a perfectly smooth octave, the reason for this necessity remained entirely unknown, and nothing but the vaguest and most fanciful suggestions were offered to account for it—such as, for instance, that "the human mind delights in simple numerical relations." This attempt at explanation overlooked the obvious fact that many people who knew nothing either about vibrations or the delights of simple numerical relations, could tell a perfect octave from an imperfect one a great deal better than the majority of men of science. The true explanation, which it was left for Helmholtz to discover, lies in the fact, that *only by exactly satisfying the assigned numerical relation, can the partial-tones of the higher clang be brought into exact coincidence with partial-tones of the lower, and thus all beats and consequent dissonance prevented.*

82. No narrower interval than an octave can be found which gives an *absolutely* perfect concord.

The nearest approach to such a concord is the Fifth.

Here we get two pairs of coincidences 3—2 and 6—4, but a certain roughness is caused by 3 of the higher clang being within beating-distance of both 4 and 5 of the lower clang. The tuning must be perfectly accurate, this interval being closely bounded by harsh discords. The result of an error of a semitone is as follows :—

For every single vibration per second by which the higher clang is out, there will be two beats per second from the pair 3—2 with others of greater rapidity, but less intensity, from the higher pairs. The result, for the Fifth, is, therefore, that, however accurately tuned, it involves an appreciable roughness. It is true that since 4 and 5 are generally weak, and the beating intervals are whole tones, the roughness will be very slight: still the trace of dissonance due to it prevents our classing the Fifth as an interval quite equally smooth with the octave.

83. For the Fourth we have

The amount of dissonance is greater than in the case of the Fifth, since 3 and 2 are usually *both* powerful tones, and produce therefore louder beats than those of 4—3 and 5—3. There are, in addition, the beating pairs 6—4 and 6—5. Moreover the first pair of coincident or partial tones, 4—3, are, in general, *weaker* than the beating pair below them, 3—2. The Fourth is bounded only on one side by a harsh discord. If its upper clang is half a note too sharp, we have the interval C—$F\sharp$, which is treated in the last figure but one. Slight flattening of the F will set the pair 4—3 beating slowly; the disappearance of their beats thus secures the accurate tuning of the interval. On the other hand, lowering F weakens the beats of 3—2, by widening the distance between those tones, and, therefore, tends to lessen the whole amount of roughness. These considerations go far to explain the fact that a long dispute runs through the history of music, as to whether the Fourth ought to be treated as a concord or as a discord. The decision ultimately arrived at in favour of the first of these alternatives was perhaps, as Helmholtz suggests, due more to the fact that the Fourth is the inversion of the Fifth, than to the inherent smoothness of the former interval.

84. Next come the intervals of the Major Third and Major Sixth, which shall be taken together, as they are very nearly equally consonant.

The dissonance due to the pair 3—2, separated by a tone in the Sixth, is perhaps, about equal to that of the weaker pair 4—3, which are only a semi-tone apart, in the Third. The definition of these intervals depending, as it does (in both) on the *fifth* tone of the lower clang, will in general be but feebly marked.

85. The last remaining intervals, less than an octave, which rank as concords, are those of the Minor Third and Minor Sixth.

Each contains strong elements of dissonance; in

fact, we are here near the boundary line between concord and discord. As regards sharpness of definition,

the tones 6 and 5, on which it depends in the first of the two intervals, are, in the sounds of most instruments, weak or even entirely absent, while for the second interval the series of partial-tones must be extended as far as the 8th of the lower clang in order to reach the first coincident pair. Accordingly the Minor Sixth can hardly be said to be defined *at all*, for clangs of ordinary quality, by coincidence of partial-tones. Its powerful beating pair 3—2, separated by the interval of greatest dissonance, a semi-tone, makes it the roughest of all the concords. On the pianoforte, and other instruments with fixed tones, *the same notes (C A♭) which represent the Minor Sixth have also to do duty as one of the harshest discords, the Sharp Fifth, (C G♯).* The extremely defective consonance of the Minor Sixth could hardly be more conclusively shown than by the fact just mentioned.

86. As regards the dissonant intervals of the scale, we have, in addition to those incidentally examined above, the semi-tone, tone, and Minor

Seventh. The first two need not be examined, since obviously each pair of corresponding overtones are brought within the same beating intervals as the two fundamentals. The dissonance resulting is, of course, harsher for the half than for the whole tone. The Minor Seventh is constituted thus:

It is the mildest of the discords, in fact, in actual smoothness it decidedly surpasses the Minor Sixth.

87. In order that the reader may see at a glance the whole result of this somewhat laborious discussion, we subjoin a graphical representation of the amount of dissonance contained in the several intervals of the scale. The figure is taken, with some slight alterations, from that given at p. 519 of Helmholtz's work. The intervals, reckoned from C, are denoted by distances measured along the horizontal straight line. The dissonance for each interval is represented by the vertical distance of the curved line from the corresponding point on the horizontal line. The calculations on which the curve is based were made by Helmholtz for two constituent clangs of the quality of the violin. For pianoforte sounds the form of

the curve would be slightly different; for those of stopped organ-pipes, &c. very different indeed.

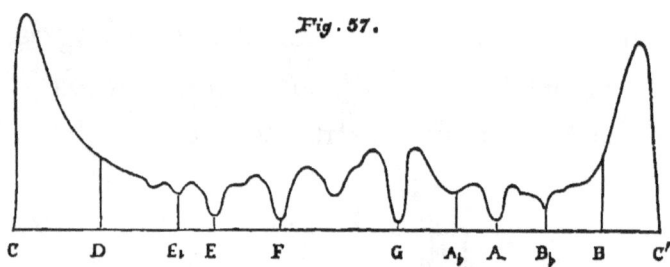
Fig. 57.

The figure indicates the sharpness of definition of an interval by the steepness with which the curve ascends in its vicinity. If we regarded the outline as that of a mountain-chain, the discords would be represented by *peaks*, and the concords by *passes*. The lowness and narrowness of a particular pass would measure the smoothness and definition of the corresponding musical interval.

88. The theory of musical consonance and dissonance, our examination of which is now concluded, necessarily leads us to regard the distinctions between different concords laid down by theoretical musicians as not in themselves absolute, but dependent on the quality of the sounds experimented upon. The results we have arrived at are generally true for sounds containing the first six partial-tones, but they will not apply, without modification, to clangs differently constituted. To take a case or

two in point. Suppose, for instance, we are dealing with sounds such as those of stopped organ-pipes which contain *only odd partial-tones* (p. 121). It is at once clear from p. 169 that the interval of the Sharp Fourth $C—F\sharp$, which owes its dissonant character to the beating pairs 3—2, 4—3, and 6—4, will become something quite different when the dissonance due to all these pairs disappears, as it must do, since each of them contains at least *one* partial-tone of an *even* order. The Minor Sixth would also gain in smoothness in such a *timbre*, by the removal of the loudly discordant pair 3—2.

Helmholtz has examined the case of a hautbois taking one note of an interval and a clarionet the other, and shown that some concords sound best when the former instrument plays the upper note and the latter the lower, while with others the reverse is the case. The hautbois produces the uninterrupted series of partial-tones, the clarionet only its odd members. Reference to p. 171 shows that, in the case of the Major Third, we can only get rid of the dissonant pair 4—3 by assigning the higher note to the hautbois. The Fourth, on the contrary, will be seen, by p. 170, to sound smoothest when the clarionet is above the hautbois, since by this arrangement we divorce the quarrelsome couple 3—2, whose bickerings will, in the opposite position, continue to be heard. These conclusions, which experiment confirms, are, I believe, in advance of any obtained empirically by musical theorists. Corresponding rules might easily be elicited for other instruments.

89. It is possible to draw from the general theory of consonance and dissonance an inference which seems, at first sight, fatal to the truth of the theory itself. "If," it may be said, "the difference between a consonant and a dissonant interval depends entirely on the behaviour towards each other of certain pairs of overtones; then, in the case of sounds like those of large stopped flue-pipes, *where there are no overtones at all*, the distinction between concords and discords ought entirely to disappear, and the interval of a Seventh, for instance, to sound just as smooth as that of an octave. As this is notoriously not the fact, the theory cannot be true."

In order to meet this objection, it will be necessary first to acquaint the reader with certain known experimental facts which Helmholtz has dragged out of the obscurity in which they had lain for fully a century, and forced to deliver their testimony in favour of his theory.

90. Let two tuning-forks of different pitch mounted on their respective resonance-boxes, and therefore producing simple tones, be thrown into

powerful vibration by the use of a resined fiddle-bow. With adequate attention, it is possible to recognize, in addition to the tones of the forks themselves, certain new sounds, which usually differ in pitch from *both* the former ones. These tones, called, from the manner of their production, *combination-tones*, fall into two classes, with only one of which, discovered in 1740 by a German organist named *Sorge*, we need here concern ourselves. It consists of a series of tones called combination-tones of the *first, second, third, &c., orders*, of which the *first* is of the most importance, as it can be heard without difficulty. Its pitch is determined by the following law. *The combination-tone of the first order of two simple primary-tones has for its vibration-number the difference between the respective vibration-numbers of the primaries.* Thus, e.g., if the two primaries make 200 and 300 vibrations per second, and therefore form a Fifth with each other, the first combination-tone will make 100 vibrations per second, and, accordingly, lie exactly one octave below the graver of the two primary tones. In this manner we can determine the combination-tones of the first order for pairs of simple primaries forming any given interval with each other. The following table, copied from Helmholtz's work, shows the results for all the consonant intervals not exceeding one octave.

Interval.	Vibration-ratio.	Difference.	Depth of the Combination-tone below the graver primary.
Octave	1 : 2	1	Unison
Fifth	2 : 3	1	Octave
Fourth	3 : 4	1	Twelfth
Major Third	4 : 5	1	Two Octaves
Minor Third	5 : 6	1	Two Octaves & Major Third
Major Sixth	3 : 5	2	Fifth
Minor Sixth	5 : 8	3	Major Sixth

In musical notation the same thing stands thus, the primaries being denoted by minims, and the combination-tones by crotchets.

Combination-tones are produced with remarkable distinctness by the harmonium. If the primaries shown in the treble stave are played on that instrument while the pressure of air in the bellows is vigorously sustained, the corresponding combination-tones of the first order, written in the bass, come out with unmistakeable clearness. They are in fact much better heard thus than from tuning-forks.

Combination-tones of the *second order* may be treated as if they were first-order tones produced between one or other of the primaries and the combination-tone of the first order. Similarly we may regard each combination-tone of the *third order* as due to a second-order tone, paired either with one of the primaries, with the first-order tone or with its own fellow of the second order. Successive subtraction will therefore enable us to determine the vibration-number of a combination-tone of any order from the vibration numbers of the two primaries.

Combination-tones grow rapidly feebler as their order becomes higher. Those of the first order are usually distinct enough, and those of the second to be heard with a little trouble. The third order is only recognizable when entire stillness is secured, and the greatest attention paid. It is a moot point whether the fourth-order tones can be heard at all.

91. We can now show that the existence of combination-tones prevents intervals formed by two simple tones from altogether lacking the characteristic differences of consonance and dissonance, though those differences are far less marked than in the case of composite sounds. To begin with the octave. Let us suppose that we have two simple tones forming nearly this interval, but that the higher of them

is a little sharp, so that the octave is not strictly in tune, is in fact slightly *impure*. Let the lower tone make 100, the higher 201, vibrations per second. They will give rise to a combination-tone making 101 vibrations per second (p. 177), and this with the lower primary will produce *one beat per second*. If the higher primary had been flat, instead of sharp, making, say, 199 vibrations per second, we should have had 99, as combination-tone, giving rise, with 100, to beats of the same rapidity as before. These beats cannot be got rid of except by making the vibration-ratio exactly $1:2$, i.e. the octave perfectly pure. The roughness must increase both when the interval widens and when it contracts, so that' the octave, in simple tones, is a well-defined concord bounded on either side by decided discords. This result may be easily verified experimentally by taking two tuning-forks forming an octave with each other, and throwing the interval slightly out of tune by causing a pellet of wax to adhere to a prong of one of them. On exciting the forks the beats will be distinctly heard.

The octave is the only interval which is defined by the beats of a combination-tone of the first order with one of the primary tones. For the next smoothest concord, that of the Fifth, we are obliged to have recourse to the second order. Thus, proceeding as in the case of the octave, we have

Primaries	200	301
C. T. of 1st order		101
C. Ts. of 2nd order	99	200
No. of beats per sec.		2

The Fifth is, thus, a fairly well-defined consonance, though decidedly less sharply bounded than the octave, owing to the feebleness of the C. T. of 2nd order. For the Fourth we have

Primaries	300		401
C. T. of 1st order		101	
C. Ts. of 2nd order	199		300
C. Ts. of 3rd order	101	202	98
No. of beats per sec.		3	

The 3rd-order tone being excessively weak, the interval of a Fourth can scarcely be said to be defined at all. Still less can the remaining consonant intervals of the scale, by the evanescent beats of still higher orders of combination-tones.

92. With simple-tones, then, the case stands thus. The intervals of a Second and a Major-Seventh are palpably dissonant, owing to the beats of the primaries, in the former, and of a first-order combination-tone with a primary, in the latter. There is a certain amount of dissonance in intervals slightly

narrower or slightly wider than a Fifth, but of a feebler kind than in the case of the octave, inasmuch as it is due to only a second-order combination-tone. Whatever dissonance may exist near the Fourth is practically imperceptible. All other intervals are free from dissonance. Accordingly all intervals from the Minor Third nearly up to the Fifth, and from a little above the Fifth up to the Major Seventh, ought to sound equally smooth. This conclusion is probably very inconsistent with the views of musical theorists, who regard concord and discord as entirely independent of quality, but it is strictly borne out by experiment. With the tones of tuning-forks the intervals lying between the Minor and Major Thirds, and between the Minor and Major Sixths, though sounding somewhat *strange*, are entirely free from roughness, and, therefore, cannot be described as dissonant. As a further verification of this fact, Helmholtz advises such of his readers as have access to an organ to try the effect of playing alternately the smoothest concords and the most extreme discords which the musical scale contains, on stops yielding only simple-tones, such, e.g., as the flute, or stopped diapason. The vivid contrasts which such a proceeding calls out on instruments of bright *timbre*, like the pianoforte and harmonium, or the more brilliant stops of the organ, such as principal, hautbois, trumpet, &c., are here blurred and effaced, and everything sounds dull and inanimate, in consequence. Nothing can show more decisively than such an experiment that the presence of over-tones confers on music its most characteristic charms.

Thus the remark put into the mouth of a supposed objector in § 89 turns out to be no objection whatever to Helmholtz's theory of consonance and dissonance, but, so far as it represents actual facts, to be valid against the prevalent views of musical theorists.

93. It may we well to advert briefly, in this place, to a point connected with combination-tones which may otherwise occur as a difficulty to the reader's mind. When two clangs coexist, combination-tones are produced between every pair which can be formed of a tone from one clang with a tone from the other. These intrusive tones will usually be very numerous, and, for aught that appears, may interfere with those originally present, to such an extent as to render useless a theory based on the presence of partial-tones only. Helmholtz has removed any such apprehension, by showing that, in general, *dissonance due to combination-tones produced between overtones, never exists except where it is already present by virtue of direct action among the overtones themselves.* Thus the only effect attri-

butable to this source is a somewhat increased roughness in all intervals except absolutely perfect concords. No modifications, therefore, have to be introduced, on this score, in the conclusions of §§ 81—86.

CHAPTER IX.

ON CONSONANT TRIADS.

94. In the ensuing portion of this enquiry we shall have to make more frequent use than hitherto of vibration-fractions. It may, therefore, be well to explain the rules for their employment, in order that the student may acquire some facility in handling them. The vibration-fraction of an assigned interval expresses the ratio of the numbers of vibrations performed *in the same time* by the two notes which form the interval. The particular length of time chosen is a matter of absolute indifference. The upper note of an octave, for instance, vibrates twice as often as the lower does in any time we choose to select, be it an hour, a minute, a second, or a part of a second. It is often convenient to determine the vibration-fraction of an interval from the vibration-numbers of its constituent notes: in such a case we choose *one second* as our time of comparison, and in this way vibration-fractions were

defined in § 34: any other standard is however equally legitimate, though, in general, less convenient. To illustrate these remarks on a particular case, the vibration-fraction $\frac{5}{4}$ indicates that, while the lower of two notes forming a Major Third makes four vibrations, the higher of them makes five. Therefore, while the lower makes one vibration, the higher makes $\frac{5}{4}$ths of a vibration, or $1\frac{1}{4}$ vibrations. Conversely, while the higher note makes one vibration, the lower makes $\frac{4}{5}$ths of a vibration. The same reasoning being equally applicable to other cases, it follows that any fraction greater than unity denotes the number of vibrations, and fractions of a vibration, made by the higher of two notes forming a certain interval, while the lower note is making a single vibration. Similarly, any fraction less than unity indicates the proportion of a whole vibration performed by the lower note, while the upper is making one complete vibration.

The rules for adding and subtracting intervals shall next be laid down.

95. Suppose that, starting from a given note, a second note, a Fifth above it, is sounded, and then a third note, a Major Third above the second. What will be the vibration-fraction of the interval formed by the first and third notes, i. e. of the sum of a Fifth and a Major Third? We will, for short-

ness, call the three notes (1), (2), (3) in order of ascending pitch. The vibration-fractions being, for (1)—(2), $\frac{3}{2}$, and, for 2— 3, $\frac{5}{4}$, we proceed thus :

While (2) makes 4 vibrations, (3) makes 5 vibrations.
Therefore, while (2) makes 1 vibration, (3) makes $\frac{5}{4}$ vibrations.
Therefore, while (2) makes 3 vibrations, (3) makes $3 \times \frac{5}{4}$ vibrations.
But while (2) makes 3 vibrations, (1) makes 2 vibrations.
Therefore, while (1) makes 2 vibrations, (3) makes $3 \times \frac{5}{4}$ vibrations.
Therefore, while (1) makes 1 vibration, (3) makes $\frac{3}{2} \times \frac{5}{4}$ vibrations.

Our result, then, is *the two vibration-numbers multiplied together*. The reasoning is perfectly general, and gives us the following rule.

To find the vibration-fraction for the sum of two intervals, multiply their separate vibration-fractions together.

96. Next, take the opposite case. Let (2) be a Major Third above (1), and (3) a Fifth above (1), and let the vibration-fraction for the interval (2)—(3) be required.

While (1) makes 4 vibrations, (2) makes 5 vibrations.
Therefore, while (1) makes 1 vibration, (2) makes $\frac{5}{4}$ vibrations.
But, while (1) makes 2 vibrations, (3) makes 3 vibrations.
Therefore, while (1) makes 1 vibration, (3) makes $\frac{3}{2}$ vibrations.
Hence, while (2) makes $\frac{5}{4}$ vibrations, (3) makes $\frac{3}{2}$ vibrations.
Therefore, while (2) makes $\frac{1}{5}$ of a vibration, (3) makes $\frac{1}{5} \times \frac{3}{2}$ of a vibration.
Therefore, while (2) makes 1 vibration, (3) makes $\frac{4}{5} \times \frac{3}{2}$ vibrations.

The result here is *the quotient resulting from the division of the larger vibration-fraction by the smaller:* hence we have this general rule.

To find the vibration-fraction for the difference of two intervals, divide the vibration-fraction of the wider by that of the narrower interval.

Thus *multiplication and division of vibration-fractions* correspond to *addition and subtraction of intervals*[1].

97. One of the simplest cases of our second rule occurs when an interval has to be inverted. The 'inversion' of any assigned interval narrower than an octave is the difference between it and an octave, i.e. the interval which remains after the first has been subtracted from an octave. Thus to find the vibration-number for the inversion of the Minor Third we merely have to divide 2 by $\frac{6}{5}$, or in other words *invert the vibration-fraction of the interval and multiply by* 2. This applies to all cases. In the particular example selected, the result is $\frac{5}{3}$; the inversion of the Minor Third is therefore the Major Sixth. The relation between an interval and its inversion is obviously mutual, so that each may be

[1] By simply reducing the numerical results, obtained in §§ 95, 96, the student will establish the following propositions:

'A Major Third added to a Fifth produces a Major Seventh.'

'A Major Third subtracted from a Fifth leaves a Minor Third.'

described as the inversion of the other. Accordingly the inversion of the Major Sixth is the Minor Third.

The following table shows the three pairs of consonant intervals narrower than an octave, which stand to each other in the mutual relation of inversions.

$$\text{Minor Third} \quad (\tfrac{6}{5}) \text{—Major Sixth } (\tfrac{5}{3})$$
$$\text{Major Third} \quad (\tfrac{5}{4}) \text{—Minor Sixth } (\tfrac{8}{5})$$
$$\text{Fourth } (\tfrac{4}{3}) \text{—Fifth } (\tfrac{3}{2})$$

The student is advised to verify, by the method of p. 188, the fact that each of these intervals is the inversion of that placed by its side.

98. A combination of musical sounds of different pitch is called a 'chord.' Hitherto we have considered only chords of two notes, or 'binary' chords. We now go on to chords of three notes, or, as they are usually called, 'triads.' A binary chord is, of course, consonant if its two notes form a consonant interval. A triad contains *three* intervals, one between its extreme notes, and one between the middle note and *each* of the other two. In order that the chord may be free from dissonance, those intervals must *all three* be concords.

99. We may, then, search for consonant triads in the following manner. Having selected the lowest of the three notes at pleasure, choose two others, each of which forms *with the bottom note* a consonant

interval. Next, examine whether the interval formed by the last chosen notes *with each other* is also a concord. If so, the triad itself is consonant. In order to determine all the consonant triads within an octave above the fixed bottom note, we must assign to the middle and top notes every possible consonant position with respect to the bottom note, and reject all such relative positions as give rise to dissonant intervals between those notes themselves. The remaining positions will constitute all the consonant triads which have for their lowest note that originally selected. The intervals at our disposal are, for the middle note, from the Minor Third to the Minor Sixth, and, for the upper note, from the Major Third to the Major Sixth.

In the annexed table[1] the possible positions of the middle note with respect to the bottom note, are shown in the left-hand vertical column, the name of each interval being accompanied by its vibration-fraction. The possible positions of the top note are similarly shown in the highest horizontal column. Each space common to a horizontal and a vertical column contains the vibration-fraction of the interval formed between the simultaneous positions of the middle and upper notes named at their extremities. Where

[1] This table is copied with slight modifications from Helmholtz's work.

these intervals are dissonant, their vibration-fractions are enclosed in square brackets. When they are concords the name of the interval is, in each case, appended.

	Major Third $\frac{5}{4}$	Fourth $\frac{4}{3}$	Fifth $\frac{3}{2}$	Minor Sixth $\frac{8}{5}$	Major Sixth $\frac{5}{3}$
Minor Third $\frac{6}{5}$	$\left[\frac{25}{24}\right]$	$\left[\frac{10}{9}\right]$	$\frac{5}{4}$ Major Third	$\frac{4}{3}$ Fourth	$\left[\frac{25}{0}\right]$
Major Third $\frac{5}{4}$		$\left[\frac{16}{15}\right]$	$\frac{6}{5}$ Minor Third	$\left[\frac{32}{25}\right]$	$\frac{4}{3}$ Fourth
Fourth $\frac{4}{3}$			$\left[\frac{9}{8}\right]$	$\frac{6}{5}$ Minor Third	$\frac{5}{4}$ Major Third
Fifth $\frac{3}{2}$				$\left[\frac{16}{15}\right]$	$\left[\frac{10}{9}\right]$
Minor Sixth $\frac{8}{5}$					$\left[\frac{25}{24}\right]$

100. The following, then, are all the cases:

Middle Note.	Upper Note.
Minor Third	Fifth, or Minor Sixth
Major Third	Fifth, or Major Sixth
Fourth	Minor Sixth, or Major Sixth

or, in musical notation,

They give us two groups of three *major*, and three *minor*, triads, which may be arranged thus:

(a) {Fifth. / Major Third.} (b) {Minor Sixth. / Minor Third.} (c) {Major Sixth. / Fourth.}

(α) {Fifth. / Minor Third.} (β) {Major Sixth. / Major Third.} (γ) {Minor Sixth. / Fourth.}

101. Instead of defining our six consonant triads, as we have done, by the intervals formed by their middle and top notes with the bottom note, we may define them by the intervals separating the middle from the bottom note, and the top from the middle note. In order to make this change we have, in each case, a process of subtraction of intervals to perform. Thus the difference between a Fifth and a Major Third is $\frac{3}{2} \times \frac{4}{5}$, i.e. $\frac{6}{5}$, or a Minor Third.

Proceeding in this way, we find that the top and middle notes are separated by the following intervals:

(a)	(b)	(c)	(α)	(β)	(γ)
Minor Third	Fourth	Major Third	Major Third	Fourth	Minor Third

INVERSION OF TRIADS.

Hence we may write our two groups as follows:

$(a')\begin{cases}\text{Minor Third.}\\ \text{Major Third.}\end{cases}$ $(b')\begin{cases}\text{Fourth.}\\ \text{Minor Third.}\end{cases}$ $(c')\begin{cases}\text{Major Third.}\\ \text{Fourth.}\end{cases}$

$(\alpha')\begin{cases}\text{Major Third.}\\ \text{Minor Third.}\end{cases}$ $(\beta')\begin{cases}\text{Fourth.}\\ \text{Major Third.}\end{cases}$ $(\gamma')\begin{cases}\text{Minor Third.}\\ \text{Fourth.}\end{cases}$

It will now be easy to show that the triads of each group are very closely connected together. Take (a'), and let us form another triad from it, by causing its bottom note to ascend one octave, the other two remaining where they were. The middle will then become the bottom note, the top the middle note, and the octave of the former bottom note the top note. Hence the lower interval of the new triad will be the upper interval of the old one, i.e. a Minor Third. The upper interval of the new triad will necessarily be the *inversion of the interval which separated the extreme notes of the old triad*. This interval is a Fifth [see (a), p. 192], and its inversion, by the table on p. 189, is a Fourth. Hence the new triad is $\begin{Bmatrix}\text{Fourth,}\\ \text{Minor Third,}\end{Bmatrix}$ which is identical with (b').

If we modify (b') in the same way, the new interval is the inversion of the Minor Sixth, i.e. the Major Third, and the resulting triad, viz. $\begin{Bmatrix}\text{Major Third}\\ \text{Fourth,}\end{Bmatrix}$ is identical with (c'). This triad, when

T.

similarly treated, brings us back to (a'), and the cycle of changes is complete. By an extension of the word 'inversion,' it is usual to call the triads (b') and (c') the *first and second inversions of the triad* (a').

Exactly similar relations hold between the members of the second group of triads: (β') and (γ') are, accordingly, called the first and second inversions of the triad (a). The proof is exactly like that just given, and will be easily supplied by the reader.

102. If we choose C as the bottom note of (a') and (a'), the major and minor groups will be expressed in musical notation by

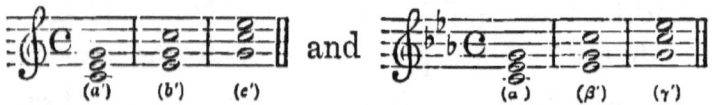

They may also be defined in the language of Thorough Bass, which refers every chord to its lowest note, in accordance with the mode adopted in (a), (b), (c); (a), (β), (γ). Thus the triads (a'), (b'), (c') would be indicated by the figures $\frac{5}{3}$, $\frac{6}{3}$, $\frac{6}{4}$ respectively, and *so would the triads* (a') (β') (γ'); the differences between Minor and Major Thirds and Sixths being left to be indicated by the key-signature.

The positions (a') and (a') are regarded as the fundamental ones of each group, (b') (c') and (β') (γ')

being treated as derived from them respectively by inversion.

103. The fundamental triads bear the name of their lowest notes, thus (a') and (a') are called respectively the major and minor *common-chords of C*.

The remaining members of each group are not named after their own lowest note, but after that of their fundamental inversion; thus (b') (c') and (β') (γ') are respectively major and minor common-chords of C *in their first and second inversions*.

The reason of this, as far as the major group is concerned, follows, directly from Helmholtz's theory of consonance and dissonance. The notes of the triads (a'), (b'), (c') are all coincident with individual *overtones* of a clang whose fundamental-tone is the low C, [musical notation] for (a') and (b'), and the octave above that note for (c'): hence they may be regarded as forming a part of the clang of a C-sound, and therefore each triad may be appropriately called by its name. With the Minor triads this is not so completely true, because the $E\flat$ in (a'), (β'), (γ') is not coincident with an overtone of C. The other two notes, however, are in each case leading partial-tones of the clang of C, and therefore these triads belong at any rate more to C than to any other note.

Common-chords of more than three constituent sounds can only be formed by adding to the consonant triads notes which are exact octaves above or below those of the triads.

104. The marked distinction existing, for every musical ear, between the bright open character of major, and the gloomy veiled effect of minor chords, is attributed by Helmholtz to the different way in which combination-tones enter in the two cases. The positions of the first-order combination-tones, for each of the six consonant triads, are shown in crotchets in the appended stave, the primaries being indicated by minims. Each interval gives rise to its own combination-tone, but, in the cases of the fundamental position and second inversion of the C-Major triad, two combination-tones happen to coincide. The reader will at once notice that in the major group no note extraneous to the harmony is brought in by the combination-tones. In the minor group this is no longer the case. The fundamental position, and the first inversion, of the triad, both bring in an $A\flat$, which is foreign to the harmony, and the second inversion involves an additional extraneous note, $B\flat$. The position of these adventitious sounds is not such as to produce *dissonance*, for which they are too far apart from each other and from the notes of the triad; but they cloud the transparency of the har-

mony, and so give rise to the effects characteristic of the minor mode.

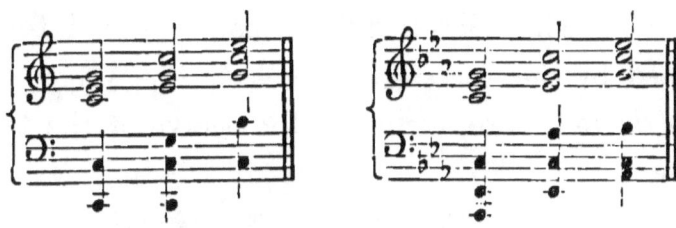

The unsatisfying character of Minor, compared with Major, triads, comes out with peculiar distinctness on the harmonium; as indeed, from the powerful combination-tones of that instrument, we should naturally have anticipated.

CHAPTER X.

ON PURE INTONATION AND TEMPERAMENT.

105. The vibration-fractions of the intervals formed by the successive notes of the Major scale *with the tonic*, are, including the octave of the tonic, these:

$$\tfrac{9}{8},\ \tfrac{5}{4},\ \tfrac{4}{3},\ \tfrac{3}{2},\ \tfrac{5}{3},\ \tfrac{15}{8},\ 2.$$

The intervals *between successive notes of the scale* are determined by dividing each of these fractions by that which precedes it. Thus the consecutive intervals of the Major scale come out as follows:

C		D		E		F		G		A		B		C'
	$\tfrac{9}{8}$		$\tfrac{10}{9}$		$\tfrac{16}{15}$		$\tfrac{9}{8}$		$\tfrac{10}{9}$		$\tfrac{9}{8}$		$\tfrac{16}{15}$	

Only three different intervals are obtained. $\tfrac{9}{8}$ is slightly wider than $\tfrac{10}{9}$; $\tfrac{16}{15}$ decidedly narrower than the other two. $\tfrac{9}{8}$ and $\tfrac{10}{9}$ are called whole tones, $\tfrac{16}{15}$ a half-tone or semi-tone, though, strictly speaking, two intervals of this width added together somewhat exceed the greater of the two whole tones; since $\tfrac{16}{15} \times \tfrac{16}{15}$ or $\tfrac{256}{225}$ is to $\tfrac{9}{8}$ in the ratio of 2048 to 2025.

Suppose we had a keyed instrument containing a number of octaves, each divided into seven notes, forming the ordinary scale as above : any music could be played on it which did not introduce notes foreign to the key of C Major. But now, suppose we wanted to be able to play in *another* Major key as well as in that of C, for instance G. It would be necessary for this purpose to introduce two new notes in every octave of the key-board. If G is the new tonic, A will not serve as the second of its scale, because the step between tonic and second is, not $\frac{10}{9}$, but $\frac{9}{8}$. Hence we must have a fresh note lying between A and B. Further, F will not do for the seventh of the scale of G, as it is separated from G by $\frac{9}{8}$, instead of $\frac{16}{15}$. This necessitates a second additional note lying between F and G. If we take, as our original octave, that from middle-C upwards, we have the following vibration-numbers :

C	D	E	F	G	A	B	C'
264	297	330	352	396	440	495	528

The new notes, being respectively $\frac{9}{8}$ *above*, and $\frac{16}{15}$ *below* G, have for their vibration-numbers $\frac{9}{8} \times 396$ and $\frac{15}{16} \times 396$, i.e. $445\frac{1}{2}$ and $371\frac{1}{4}$. The other notes of the scale of G Major can be supplied from that of C Major. Hence these two scales are closely connected with each other. Another key nearly related to the key of *C* is that of *F*. Its Fourth is $\frac{4}{3} \times 352$, or $469\frac{1}{3}$, which falls between *A* and *B*. Its Major Sixth is $\frac{5}{3} \times 352$, or $586\frac{2}{3}$, which is clearly not an exact octave of any note between *C* and *C'*. The corresponding note in our octave, found by division by 2, is $293\frac{1}{3}$, which comes between *C* and *D*. Thus, two more new notes in the octave must be introduced, to make the key of *F* major attainable.

106. In order that the reader may see, at a glance, the variety of sounds which are requisite to supply complete Major scales for the seven keys of *C, D, E, F, G, A* and *B*, the vibration-numbers for all the notes of these scales are calculated out and exhibited in the following table.

Reducing those notes which lie beyond the

Tonic	Second	Major Third	Fourth	Fifth	Major Sixth	Major Seventh
C, 264	297	330	352	396	440	495
D, 297	$334\frac{1}{8}$	$371\frac{1}{4}$	396	$445\frac{1}{2}$	495	$556\frac{7}{8}$
E, 330	$371\frac{1}{4}$	$412\frac{1}{2}$	440	495	550	$618\frac{3}{4}$
F, 352	396	440	$469\frac{1}{3}$	528	$586\frac{2}{3}$	660
G, 396	$445\frac{1}{2}$	495	528	594	660	$742\frac{1}{2}$
A, 440	495	550	$586\frac{2}{3}$	660	$733\frac{1}{3}$	825
B, 495	$556\frac{7}{8}$	$618\frac{3}{4}$	660	$742\frac{1}{2}$	825	$928\frac{1}{8}$

octave, by dividing them by 2, and arranging the results in order of magnitude, we have *twelve notes* foreign to the scale of C Major, the positions of which, with reference to the notes of that scale, are as follows:

C, 275, $278\frac{7}{16}$, $293\frac{1}{3}$, D, $309\frac{3}{8}$, E, $334\frac{1}{8}$, F, $366\frac{2}{3}$, $371\frac{1}{4}$, G, $412\frac{1}{2}$, $417\frac{1}{2}$, A, $445\frac{1}{2}$, $464\frac{1}{16}$, $469\frac{1}{3}$, B.

107. If it is desired to be able to play in the *Minor* mode of each of the seven keys, as well as in the *Major*, additional notes will be called for. Each scale must contain three Minor intervals, viz. Minor Third, Minor Sixth, and Minor Seventh. The following subsidiary table exhibits the vibration-numbers of the sounds forming these intervals with the successive key-notes.

Tonic	Minor Third	Minor Sixth	Minor Seventh
C, 264	$316\frac{4}{5}$	$422\frac{2}{5}$	$469\frac{1}{3}$
D, 297	$356\frac{2}{5}$	$475\frac{1}{5}$	528
E, 330	396	528	$586\frac{2}{3}$
F, 352	$422\frac{2}{5}$	$563\frac{1}{5}$	$625\frac{7}{9}$
G, 396	$475\frac{1}{5}$	$633\frac{1}{5}$	704
A, 440	528	704	$782\frac{2}{9}$
B, 495	594	792	880

Reducing these to one octave, as before, we find *seven* notes not included in the previous list, occupying the following positions:

C, $281\tfrac{3}{5}$, D, $312\tfrac{5}{9}$, $316\tfrac{4}{5}$, E, F, $356\tfrac{2}{5}$, $391\tfrac{1}{9}$, G, $422\tfrac{2}{5}$, A, $475\tfrac{1}{5}$, B.

108. Hence, to play perfectly in tune in both Major and Minor modes of the seven keys C, D, E, F, G, A, B, it is necessary to have a key-board with *twenty-six notes* in every octave. This number, large as it is, by no means includes all necessary notes. Modern music is written in *sharp* and *flat* keys, i. e. in such whose tonics are not coincident with any one of the notes $CDE...B$. Moreover, the sharp and flat key-notes are different from each other. Thus $G\sharp$, being a Major Third above E, is, as the first table shows, $412\tfrac{1}{2}$; while $A\flat$ is seen, by the second table, to be $422\tfrac{2}{5}$, which is a somewhat sharper note. As the seven keys which have been already examined require 26 notes in the octave, we may anticipate that the *ten* additional sharp and flat keys will bring in a still larger number. It is needless to institute a detailed enquiry into these scales, but, after what he has already seen, the student will feel no surprise when he learns that a competent authority[1], who has examined the

[1] Mr A. J. Ellis, *Proceedings of the Royal Society*, Vol. XIII. p. 98.

subject most minutely in reference both to melodic and harmonic requisites, fixes 72 *notes in the octave* as the number essential to theoretically complete command over *all the keys* used in modern music.

109. Without, however, assuming this result, the facts we have already ourselves established are amply sufficient to show how serious are the imperfections of tune which inevitably beset instruments with fixed tones, such as the pianoforte, harmonium and organ, containing *only twelve notes in each octave*. Pure intonation in the 'natural' keys alone, i. e. those whose tonics are white notes on the board, demands, as has been seen, more than twice this number of available sounds; and many more still, if the keys with tonics on the black notes are to be included. Perfect tuning *in all the keys* being entirely out of the question, a compromise of some kind is the only possible course. Thus we may tune a single key, say C, perfectly; in which case most of the other keys will be so out of tune as to be unbearable. Or again, we may distribute the errors over certain often-used keys, and accumulate them in others which are of less frequent occurrence.

Expedients of this kind are described as modes of 'tempering,' and the system adopted in tuning any particular instrument is called its 'temperament.' A vast number of different methods of tempering have been proposed and tried during the history of the organ and pianoforte.

110. That which has at last been almost universally adopted is the system of *equal temperament*. It consists in dividing each octave into *twelve precisely equal intervals*. Each of these intervals is called a semi-tone, and any two of them together a whole tone.

The octave of which C, 264, is the lowest note, will contain, on the equal temperament system, the following sounds. The vibration-numbers are given true to the nearest integer. When a note is slightly sharper than that so indicated, this is shown by the sign + attached to the vibration-number in question; when slightly flatter, by the sign −. For the sake of comparison, the perfect intervals of the same scale are written below the tempered ones.

C,	C♯,	D,	D♯,	E,	F,	F♯,	G,	G♯,	A,	A♯,	B
264,	280−,	296+,	314−,	333−,	352+,	373+,	395+,	419+,	444−,	470+,	498+

C,		D,	E♭,	E,	F,		G,	A♭,	A,	B♭,	B
264,		297,	317−,	330,	352,		396,	422+,	440,	469+,	495

It is clear that the regions of the tempered scale where the tuning is the most imperfect, are in the neighbourhood of the Thirds and Sixths. E and A

are nearly three vibrations per second too sharp. The Fourth and Fifth are less out of tune, in fact only wrong by a fraction of a vibration per second.

111. The intervals of the tempered scale are so nearly equal to those of the perfect scale, that, when the notes of the former are sounded *successively*, it requires a delicate ear to recognize the defective character of the tuning. When, however, more than one note is heard *at a time*, the case becomes quite different. We saw in Chapter VIII. how rigorously accurate the tuning of a consonant interval must be, to secure the greatest smoothness of which it is capable. It was also shown that such intervals are generally very closely bounded by harsh discords. Now since, in the system of equal temperament, no interval except that of the octave is accurately in tune, it follows that every representative of a concord, in its scale, must be less smooth than it would be were the tuning perfect. One of the greatest charms of music, and especially of modern music, lies in the vivid contrast presented by consonant and dissonant chords in close juxtaposition. Temperament, by impairing, even though but slightly, the perfection of the concords, necessarily somewhat weakens this contrast, and takes the edge off the musical pleasure which, in the hands of a great composer, it is capable of giving us. A fact already once adverted to

(p. 172) may be again adduced here, as illustrating the effect of temperament in blurring distinctions of consonance and dissonance, viz. that on the key-board of the pianoforte, the same two notes which represent $C\ A\flat$, which is a concord, though not a very smooth one, also appear in $C - G\sharp$, which is a decided discord. A reference to § 108 will show that, with perfect tuning, $G\sharp$ and $A\flat$ are different notes having vibration-numbers in the proportion of $412\frac{1}{2}$ to $422\frac{2}{5}$.

One of the readiest ways of recognizing the defective character of equal temperament tuning is, first, allow a few accurate voices to sing a series of sustained chords in three or four parts, without accompaniment, and then, after noticing the effect, to let them repeat the phrase while the parts are at the same time played on the pianoforte. The sour character of the concords of the accompanying instrument will be at once decisively manifested. Voices are able to sing perfect intervals, and their clear transparent concords contrast with the duller substitutes provided by the pianoforte in a way obvious to every moderately acute ear.

112. Since the voice is endowed with the power of producing all possible shades of pitch within its compass, and thus of singing absolutely pure intervals, it is clear that we ought to make the most of this great gift, and especially in the case of those

persons who are to be public singers, allow, during the years of preparation, no contact save with the purest examples of intonation. Unfortunately the practice of most singing-masters is the very reverse of this. The pupil is systematically accompanied, during vocal practice, on the pianoforte, and thus accustomed to habitual familiarity with intervals which are never strictly in tune. No one can doubt the tendency of such constant association to impair the sensitiveness to minute differences of pitch on which delicacy of musical perception depends. Evil communications are not less corrupting to good ears than to good manners. I feel convinced that we have here the reason why so comparatively few of our trained vocalists, whether amateurs or professionals, are able to sing perfectly in tune. The untutored voice of a child who has never undergone the ear-spoiling process, often gives more pleasure by the natural purity of its intonation, than the vocalization of an opera-singer who cannot keep in tune. The remedy is to practise without accompaniment, or with that of an instrument like the violin[1], which is not tied down to a few fixed sounds. Even with the

---

[1] That a violinist can play *pure* intervals has been established by Professor Helmholtz by the following decisive experiment, performed with the aid of Herr Joachim. A harmonium was employed which had been tuned so as to give pure intervals with certain stops and keys; and tempered intervals with others. A

pianoforte something might be done, by having it, when intended to be used only in assisting vocal practice, put into perfect tune in one single key, and using that key only.

The services of such an instrument would, no doubt, be comparatively very restricted, but this might not be without a corresponding advantage, if the vocalist were thereby compelled to rely a little more on his own unaided ear, lay aside his corks, and swim out boldly into the ocean of Sound.

113. The musical notation in ordinary use evidently takes for granted a scale consisting of a limited number of fixed sounds. Moreover, it indicates, directly, *absolute pitch*, and, only indirectly, *relative pitch*. In order to ascertain the interval between any two notes on the stave, we must go through a little calculation, involving the clef, the key-signature, and, perhaps, in addition, 'accidental' sharps or flats. Now these are complications, which, if necessary for pianoforte music, are perfectly gratuitous in the case of vocal music. The voice wants only to be told on what note to begin, and what *intervals* to sing afterwards, i.e. it is con-

string having been tuned in unison with a common tonic of both systems, it was found that the intervals played by the eminent violinist agreed with those of the *natural*, not with those of the *tempered* scale.

cerned with absolute pitch *only at its start*, and needs to be troubled with it no further. Hence, to place the ordinary notation before a child who is to be taught to sing, is like presenting him with a manual for learning to dance, compiled on the theory that human feet can only move in twelve different ways. Not only does the established notation encumber the vocalist with information which he does not want; it fails to communicate the one special piece of information which he *does* want. It is essential to really good music that every note heard should stand in a definite relationship to its tonic or key-note. Now, there is nothing in the established notation to mark clearly and directly what this relation ought, in each case, to be. Unless the vocalist, besides his own 'part,' is provided with that of the accompaniment, and possesses some knowledge of Harmony, he cannot ascertain how the notes set down for him are related to the key-note and to each other. The extreme inconvenience of this must have become painfully evident to any one who has frequently sung concerted music from a single part.

A Bass, we will suppose, after leaving off on $F\sharp$, is directed to rest thirteen bars, and then come in *fortissimo* on his high $E^?$. It is impossible for him to keep the absolute pitch of $F\sharp$ in his head during this long interval, which is perhaps occupied by the other voices in modulating into some remote key; and his part vouchsafes no indication in what relation the $E\flat$ stands to the notes, or chords, immediately preceding it. There remains, then, nothing for him to do but to sing, at a venture, *some* note at the top of his voice, in the hope that it may prove to be $E\flat$, though with considerable dread, in the opposite event, of the conspicuous ignominy of a fortissimo blunder.

The essential requisite for a system of vocal notation, therefore, is that, whenever it specifies any sound, it shall indicate, in a direct and simple manner, the relation in which that sound stands to its tonic for the time being. A method by which this criterion is very completely satisfied shall now be briefly described.

114. The old Italian singing-masters denoted the seven notes of the Major scale, reckoned from the key-note upwards, by the syllables

do, re, mi, fa, sol, la, si,

pronounced, of course, in the continental fashion. As long as a melody moves only in the Major mode, without modulation, it clearly admits of being written down, as far as relations of *pitch only* are concerned, by the use of these syllables. The opening phrase of 'Rule Britannia,' for instance, would stand thus:

do, do, do, re, mi, fa, sol, do, re, re, mi, fa, mi.

In order to abridge the notation, we may indicate each syllable by its initial consonant. The ambiguity which would thus arise between *sol* and *si* is got rid of by altering the latter syllable into *ti*. In order to distinguish a note from those of the same name in the adjacent octaves above and below it, an accent is added, either above or below the corresponding initial. Thus d' is an octave above d; $d_{\prime}$ an octave below d.

Where a modulation, i.e. a *change of tonic*, occurs, it is shown in the following manner. A note necessarily stands in a two-fold relation to the outgoing and the in-coming tonic. The interval it forms with the new tonic is different from that which it formed with the old one. Each of these intervals can be denoted by a suitable syllable-initial, and the displacement of one of these initials by the other, represents in the aptest manner the supersession of the old by the new tonic. The old initial is written above and to the left of the new one. Thus $^r\!f$ indicates that the note *re* is to be *sung*, but *its name changed* to *fa*. As this is a somewhat difficult point a few modulations are appended, expressed both in the established notation, and in that now under consideration. The instances selected are, from C to G; from C to F; from E to C; from G to $F\sharp$.

Immediately after a modulation, the ordinary syllable-initials come into use again, and are employed until a fresh modulation occurs. It will be seen at once, that the difficulty of 'remote keys,' which is so serious in the established notation, thus altogether disappears. For instance, a vocal phrase from Spohr's 'Last Judgment,' which in the established notation is as follows,

takes, in the notation before us, the perfectly simple form,

$$s\ l\ t\ |\ d'\ m\ f\ s\ |\ s\ f\ l\ l\ l\ s\ |\ f\ m.$$

As another example, take the following, from the same work.

115. The system of notation, of which a cursory sketch has just been given, originated, it is said, with two Norwich ladies named Glover, but has

received its present form at the hands of Mr J. Curwen, to whom it also owes the name of 'Tonic Sol-Fa,' by which it is now so widely known. As it is no part of the plan of the present work to go into technical details, only so much has been said about Mr Curwen's system as was necessary to enable the reader to grasp its essential principle. No mention has been made of the notation for Minor and Chromatic intervals, nor of that for denoting the relations of time by measures appealing directly to the eye, instead of by mere symbols. On these and all other points connected with his system, Mr Curwen's published works on Tonic Sol-Fa give full and thoroughly lucid and intelligible explanations. Mr Curwen has also created a very extensive literature of the best vocal music, printed in his own notation; given a most remarkable impulse to choral singing; and established a system of graded certificates examinations, guaranteeing the attainment, by their holders, of corresponding stages of musical cultivation.

I have enjoyed some opportunities of watching the progress of beginners taught on the old system, and on that of the Tonic Sol-Fa, and assert, without the slightest hesitation, that, as an instrument of vocal training, the new system is enormously, overwhelmingly, superior to the old. In fact, I am prepared to maintain that the complicated repulsiveness of the pitch-notation, in the old system, must be held responsible for the humiliating fact that, of the large number of musically well-endowed persons of the opulent classes who have undergone at school an elaborate instrumental and vocal training, comparatively few are able to play, and still fewer to sing, even the very simplest music *at sight*. Set an average young lady to accompany a ballad, or to sing a psalm-tune she has never seen before, and we all know what the result is likely to be. Now, there is no more inherent difficulty in teaching a child with a fairly good ear to *sing* at sight, than there is in making him *read* ordinary print at sight. A vocalist who can only sing a few elaborately prepared songs ought to be regarded as on a level with a school-boy who should be unable to read except out of his own book. If evidence be wanted to make good this assertion, it is at once to hand in the fact that the youngest children, when well trained on the Tonic Sol-Fa system, soon obtain a power of steady and accurate sight-singing, and will even tell you whether a new tune pleases them or not, after merely glancing through it, without uttering a note.

The reader will please to observe that the above remarks are strictly limited to the achievements of the Tonic Sol-Fa system in teaching *singing*. I express no opinion as to the applicability of its notation to *instrumental* music, nor do I wish to maintain that even in the vocal branch it has arrived at absolute perfection. On the contrary, I am doubtful whether its time-notation, when applied to very complicated rhythmic divisions, does not become more difficult than the system in ordinary use, and I consider the notation adopted for the Minor mode to be capable of decided improvement. On the main point, however, viz. the decisive superiority of its pitch-notation over that of the established system, and the vitally important consequences as to purity of intonation which necessarily follow from this superiority, I desire to express the most confident and uncompromising opinion.

116. In closing the enquiry which occupies the preceding chapters, it will be advisable to examine, very concisely, the bearing of our principal result, the theory of consonance and dissonance, on the æsthetics of music. Dissonance was shown to arise from rapid beats, and the concords were classed in order, according to their more or less complete freedom from dissonance; the octave coming first, followed by the Fifth, Fourth, Major Third and Sixth, and Minor Third and Sixth. This classification was strictly *physical*, depending exclusively on smooth-

ness of combined effect. On its own ground, therefore, it is absolutely unassailable, and whoever says, for instance, that a Major Third is a smoother concord than a Fifth or octave, asserts what is as demonstrably false as that the moon goes round the earth in an exact circle. Nevertheless, it by no means necessarily follows that the smoothest concords must be the most gratifying to the ear. There may be some *other* property of an interval which gives us greater satisfaction than mere consonance. Assuming, for the moment, that such a property does in fact exist, the ear, if called on to arrange the consonant intervals in the order of their *pleasantness*, might very well bring out a different arrangement from that adopted by physical science on grounds of smoothness alone. Æsthetic considerations come in here, with the same right to be heard as mechanical considerations have within their own domain.

117. Now unquestionably the ear's order of merit is *not* the same as the mechanical order. It places Thirds and Sixths first, then the Fourth and Fifth, and the octave last of all. The constant appearance of Thirds and Sixths in two-part music, compared with the infrequent employment of the remaining concords, leaves no doubt on this point. In fact these intervals have a peculiar richness and permanent charm about them, not possessed by the Fourth

or Fifth to anything like the same extent, and by the octave not at all.

The thin effect of the octave undoubtedly depends on the fact that every partial-tone of the higher of two clangs forming that interval, coincides exactly with a partial-tone of the lower clang. Thus *no new sound* is introduced by the higher clang; the quality of that previously heard is merely modified by the alteration of relative intensity among the constituent partial-tones. Major and Minor Thirds bring in a greater variety of pitch in the resulting mass of sound than does the Fifth; but this can hardly be said of the Major and Minor Sixths compared with the Fourth. On the whole, I am inclined to attribute the predilection of the ear for Thirds and Sixths, over the other concords, to circumstances connected with its perception of *key-relations*, though I am not able to give a satisfactory account of them. The ear enjoys, in alternation with consonant chords, dissonances of so harsh a description as to be barely endurable when sustained by themselves. This constitutes a marked distinction between it and the other organs of sense. A stench is not improved by alternating with the most fragrant odours, nor nauseous food rendered palatable when administered at intervals between the most delicious *plats*. A kick remains a kick, even though it be preceded and followed by caresses; and repulsive hideousness forms no welcome element in pictorial or plastic art. As instances of the kind of discords in which the ear can find delight, take the following. The chord marked * should in each case be played first *by itself*, and then in the place assigned to it by the composer. The effect of the isolated discord is so intensely harsh, that it is at first difficult to understand how any preceding and succeeding concords can make it at all tolerable; yet the sequence, in both the phrases cited, is of the rarest beauty.

Considerations such as those just alleged tend to show that, while physical science is absolutely authoritative in all that relates to the constitution of musical sounds, and the smoothness of their combinations, the composer's direct perception of what is musically beautiful must mainly direct him in the employment of his materials. It would be a serious error to force upon him a number of rules planned, on scientific principles, to secure the maximum smoothness of effect; since mere smoothness is often a matter of extremely secondary importance, compared with grandeur of harmony, and masterly movement of parts. The nature of the subject may sometimes call for a mode of treatment needing exceptional smoothness. In such a case the rules may become of considerable importance. It is well, therefore, that a composer should know and be able to handle them, but he should never allow them to fetter his freedom in wielding the higher and more spiritual weapons of his warfare.

www.ingramcontent.com/pod-product-compliance
Lightning Source LLC
Chambersburg PA
CBHW020812230426
43666CB00007B/980